VAGUS NE EXERCISE

Daily Exercise to Stimulate Vagal Tone – Overcome Anxiety and Improve General Mood

Antony Wilson

© **Copyright 2020 All rights reserved.**

This document is geared towards providing exact and reliable information with regard to the topic and issue covered. The publication is sold with the idea that the publisher is not required to render accounting, officially permitted, or otherwise, qualified services. If advice is necessary, legal or professional, a practiced individual in the profession should be ordered.

From a Declaration of Principles which was accepted and approved equally by a Committee of the American Bar Association and a Committee of Publishers and Associations.

In no way is it legal to reproduce, duplicate, or transmit any part of this document in either electronic means or in printed format. Recording of this publication is strictly prohibited and any storage of this document is not allowed unless with written permission from the publisher. All rights reserved.

The information provided herein is stated to be truthful and consistent, in that any liability, in terms of inattention or otherwise, by any usage or abuse of any policies, processes, or directions contained within is the solitary and utter responsibility of the recipient reader. Under no circumstances will any legal responsibility or blame be held against the publisher for any reparation, damages, or monetary loss due to the information herein, either directly or indirectly.

Respective authors own all copyrights not held by the publisher.

The information herein is offered for informational purposes solely and is universal as so. The presentation of the information is without a contract or any type of guarantee assurance.
The trademarks that are used are without any consent, and the publication of the trademark is without permission or backing by the trademark owner. All trademarks and brands within this book are for clarifying purposes only and are owned by the owners themselves, not affiliated with this document.

Contents

- INTRODUCTION 6
- CHAPTER 1 12
- WHAT IS THE VAGUS NERVE AND WHY IS IT SO IMPORTANT? 12
- CHAPTER 2 25
- WHERE IS THE VAGUS NERVE LOCATED? 25
- CHAPTER 3 38
- THE FUNCTIONS OF THE VAGUS NERVE 38
- CHAPTER 4 66
- EXERCISES FOR ACTIVATING THE VAGUS NERVE 66
- VAGUS NERVE YOGA 92
- BREATHING EXERCISES 109
- GETTING GREAT SLEEP 112
- COLD EXPOSURE 116
- HUMMING OR CHANTING 118
- ACTIVATING GAG REFLEX 120
- GARGLING 121
- YOGA OR PILATES 122
- MINDFULNESS PRACTICE 123
- LAUGHTER AND SOCIAL CONNECTEDNESS 125
- LISTENING TO MUSIC 126
- DAILY MOVEMENT OR EXERCISE 128
- SUNLIGHT EXPOSURE 129
- SUPPLEMENTATION 130
- PROBIOTICS 131
- OMEGA-3 FATTY ACIDS 132

5-HTP FOR SEROTONIN 133
CHAPTER 5 134
PASSIVE METHODS TO ACTIVATE THE VAGUS NERVE 134
DAILY PRACTICES FOR ACTIVATING THE VAGUS NERVE 139
CHAPTER 6 141
MEASURING VAGUS NERVE FUNCTION 141
CONCLUSION 149

INTRODUCTION

Your heart will beat 100,000 times today, without your giving it a second thought. You are going to take 23,000 breaths. Three times per minute your blood will circulate through your body and your liver will continually cleanse and detoxify that blood. The ever-changing bacteria species in your gut must collaborate symbiotically with your digestive tract to break down your food and consume the nutrients that each of your cells needs to function. Did you ever wonder how all of this happens when there is no conscious control? How do all those systems work together?

The answer to this is your autonomous nervous system. That system is a marvel of evolution. It is the part of the nervous system that, put simply, is liable for controlling unconsciously directed bodily functions.

Our bodies are built to live and survive without needing to think consciously. As humans evolved, we exponentially grew our capacity for conscious thinking. This was only possible as the systems vital for survival became subconsciously or, essentially, automatically regulated. Our forebrains have grown and let us think, contemplate and connect with the world around us. In the meantime our brainstem has managed to keep us alive and prosperous.

The brain-stem is the spinal cord's thickest and highest level. There are many information control centers within the brainstem, called nuclei, each with a specific set of functions from which it manages and sends or receives signals.

Some of these systems alert us to both internal and environmental stressors as well as risks to our survival. Whether these stressors are caused by an infection that begins to grow in our bodies, stressful thoughts about tasks that need to be completed, or the physical presence of a tiger in front of us, this system's automatically controlled functions allow us to survive. Such functions are regulated by a subset of the autonomic nervous system called the sympathetic branch (or, for convenience, sympathetic nervous system). It is known that the sympathetic nervous system increases heart rate, increases breath rate, decreases breath depth, shunts blood flow to muscles in the arms and legs and away from the liver and digestive tract, and dilates our eye pupils. In doing so, this system allows us to combat stressors or "take flight" and run away from the presenting stressors. When the sympathetic nervous system is active it is called the state of "fight-or-flight."

There is, by contrast, another branch of the autonomic nervous system that allows us to relax and recover from the day's rigor and tasks. It allows us to remain calm, lower our heart rate, lower our breath rate to take deeper, fuller breaths, and shunt blood flow away from the limbs and towards the internal organs, which allows our bodies to recover, stay calm and even procreate. This branch of the autonomic nervous system is called the parasympathetic branch (the parasympathetic nervous system, for simplicity). When the parasympathetic nervous system is involved it is termed the state of "rest-and-digest."

The vast majority of controls affirmed by the parasympathetic nervous system run through a particular pair of nerves in the body— the vagus nerve, which is the focus of this book. This is the only nerve that has its origin in the brainstem and runs through the whole body. The vagus nerve (actually the vagus nerves, since there are two paired bodies, with one on either side of the body) is responsible for regulating regulation of the heart, lungs, throat and airway muscles, liver, thyroid, pancreas, gallbladder, spleen, kidneys, small intestine, and part of the large intestine. How well the activities of the vagus nerve are a powerful determinant of health; vagus nerve dysfunction is highly associated with sickness.

Earlier we believed that nerves had a basic job: to transmit signals quickly from one area to another. We are now finding that the scope of the messages and signals conveyed by the vagus nerve is far wider and more significant than we knew initially; in addition, it is the direct link between the brain and the gut microbiome. The vagus nerve is the single most essential pathway of communication regarding digestion, nutrient status, and the ever-changing population of bacteria, viruses, yeast, parasites, and worms living within our digestive tracts.

Balance between the two branches of the autonomous nervous system is crucial in order to fully live life. Overactivation of one branch in the opposite branch may result in a significant loss of function. Chronic imbalance is what drives us down the path of dysfunction and disease. The parasympathetic organ loses its ability to function if the stress levels remain too high for too long. Blood flow and activity are centered on the sympathetic branch, suggesting blood flow to the parasympathetic branch will be restricted, and therefore function will be reduced over time. The opposite is also true, as the parasympathetic system overactivation can slow your ability to deal with potential stressors and create risks for your survival.

This is a very ubiquitous issue today, as we are living under considerable stress levels and putting huge amounts of pressure on ourselves. The capacity of our bodies to differentiate between forms of stressors has not yet developed, and mental and emotional stressors evoke the same reaction as a lion, tiger, or bear — something that threatens our life. This means we will react identically to the imminent physical danger and to our high school teacher yelling "pop quiz" or our boss sternly exclaiming that she needs to see you "immediately" in her office. Our bodies produce high levels of inflammation under consistent stress levels and are not given the opportunity to recover and rest, which is required to maintain optimal function. For this cause we break down much faster and more frequently than we used to. We are developing autoimmune diseases like rheumatoid arthritis, Hashimoto's thyroiditis and higher multiple sclerosis rates than our medical system can keep up with. We are growing all sorts of tumors and heart disease and struggling with alarmingly high rates of obesity and diabetes and our metabolism has never been higher worldwide. Our bodies can fight back and execute the tasks that our cells were built to accomplish, enabling us to overcome many of those conditions, given the right chance to recover. The problem is that too many of us don't offer our bodies this chance.

We exhaust ourselves by consuming highly processed foods (which are delivered to us through an agricultural system that is more concerned about high yields and profitability than nutritional value) and spending more time indoors, away from nature and worrying about loved ones while failing to care about oneself. In the meantime, we expect our doctors and healthcare practitioners to keep up with our life's demanding pace of change.

There is a solution to these problems: take back your own health responsibility.

Instead of depending on your doctors to monitor your wellbeing, take control back and use them as a tool to test your own hypotheses. Do your own study, learn how to manage your own stressors and find out what causes are bringing you into a depressed condition. Your primary care physicians are a very useful resource, but you're inevitably setting yourself up for failure when you hand over responsibility to a system that runs short on resources and manages hundreds and thousands of patients.

CHAPTER 1

WHAT IS THE VAGUS NERVE AND WHY IS IT SO IMPORTANT?

In simple terms, the vagus nerve is your inner nerve center's commander-in-chief, controlling all of the major organs. This is the longest cranial nerve, which ends just behind the ears in the brain and connects with all the major organs of the body. It sends fibers from your brain system to all your visceral organs, and is essentially your inner nerve center's boss, distributing nerve impulses to every organ in your body. The word vagus literally means' wanderer' as it wanders from the brain to the fertility organs throughout the body, hitting everything in between. The vagus nerve is important when it comes to mind-body communication, since it enters all of the major organs except the adrenal and thyroid glands.

This is an essential nerve to any organ with which it is in contact. It is what assists in managing brain anxiety and depression. The reason we communicate with each other is closely related to the vagus nerve as it is linked to the nerves that guide our ears to words, regulating eye contact and those that control emotions. This nerve also has the ability to affect proper release of hormones in the body which keeps our mental and physical systems healthy.

For ease of digestion in the stomach it is the vagus nerve that is responsible for increasing stomach acidity and digestive juice secretion. This can also help you absorb vitamin B12 when stimulated. If it doesn't work properly, then you can expect serious gut problems like Colitis, IBS and Re-flux, just to name a few. Reflux problems are due to a problem with the vagus nerve, because it also controls the esophagus. It's the esophagus ' unsuitable reflex which causes conditions like Gerd and Reflux.

The vagus nerve also helps control blood pressure and heart rate, preventing heart disease. While it is this nerve in the liver and pancreas that controls the balance of blood glucose, thereby preventing diabetes. The vagus nerve helps release bile when it passes through the gallbladder which is what helps your body eliminate toxins and break down fat. While in the bladder, this nerve promotes general function of the kidney, increasing blood flow, thereby improving filtration within our bodies. When the vagus nerve enters spleen, activation in all target organs may reduce inflammation. That nerve even has the power to control women's fertility and orgasms. An ineffective or blocked vagus nerve will cause havoc all over the mind and body.

Now that we know that the vagus nerve is connected to all the major organs and their proper functioning, we can easily conclude that by activating and stimulating the vagus nerve, any disorder, disease or disease of the mind, body, or spirit can be reversed or even cured. So you will actually see positive effects on issues such as anxiety disorders, heart disease, headaches and migraines, fibromyalgia, alcohol addiction, circulation, gut problems, memory problems, mood disorders, MS, and even cancer.

There are many recorded ways to activate the vagus nerve, such as singing or humming, music, yoga, meditation, breathing exercises, physical activity, and vibration just to name a few. Singing and laughing activates muscles that stimulate the nerve at the back of your throat. By addition, mild exercise and rehabilitation raises the fluid in the intestine and means the vagus nerve has been activated. Owing to the motions, a regimented yoga practice can also improve this nerve's activation, but Yoga and OMing do help stimulate the vagus nerve. All these ways of stimulating the vagus nerve you can use have one thing in common: sound!!

Doctors worldwide are finding resonant frequency of organs to help vibrate the body back into a state of health, transferring diseases such as anxiety, PTSD, migraines, depression, memory problems, chronic pain, sleep disorders, and even cancer. You can actually look at the disease as a form or disharmony,' says Dr. Gaynor, oncology director at New York's Strang-Cornell Cancer Prevention Center, and author of Sounds of Healing. We know that music and sound have profound effects on the immune system which obviously have much to do with cancer.'

In April 2016, there was also a study involving patient with Alzheimer's disease. Researchers at the University of Toronto, Wilfrid Laurier University, and the Hospitals at the Baycrest Center conducted a study of these patients at different stages of the disease, subjecting them to 40 hertz sound simulation. We acknowledged awareness, comprehension, and alertness as' promising' outcomes. Lee Bartel, one of the writers of these results, reported that,'Brain parts tend to be at the same level of communication, and that frequency is about 40 Hz. So if you have a loss like that when you have too little of that, the two parts of the brain that want to speak to each other, like the thalamus and the hippo center, the short-term memory to the long-term memory, they can't talk to each other, they won't connect, so you won't have long-term memory. Bartel clarified that the 40 Hz sound amplification therapy contributes to an 'increased frequency', which allows 'parts of the brain to talk to each other again.'

A unique school of thought comes from a French otolaryngologist, Alfred A Tomatis, who believes that the primary function of the ear is to provide electrical stimulation to all the cells of the body, thus' adjusting the entire system and giving the human being greater dynamism.' He assumes that abundant sounds in high harmonics are called charging sounds, and abundant sounds in lower tones are considered discharge signals. Tomatis claimed to have successfully treated a wide variety of diseases by speech, since they were all linked to inner ear problems. Stuttering, depression, ADD, concentration issues, and balance-related disorders were just a few of the issues he has successfully treated.

One study suggests that the Tomatis Approach is helpful of helping children with ADD. Results showed statistically significant gains for the Tomatis when opposed to the nonTomatis community: the experimental group showed significant changes in processing speed, phonological comprehension, phonemic recognition performance in hearing, actions and auditory focus.

What Does the Vagus Nerve Do?

The vagus nerve (VN) originates in the brainstem— essentially the brain trunk, which senses, processes, and regulates the vast majority of the body's automatic functions. For the most part, in order to make them happen, we do not have to consciously think about those functions. These are also autonomic functions and are regulated by the autonomic nervous system.

Some of the functions regulated by the autonomic nervous system include:

- Beating of the heart
- Blinking of eyelids

- Breath rate and depth
- Constriction and dilation of blood vessels
- Detoxification in the liver and kidneys
- Digestion in the digestive tract
- Opening and closing sweat glands
- Producing saliva and tears
- Pupil dilation and constriction in eyes
- Sexual arousal
- Urination

There are various groups of neuron cell bodies called nuclei inside the brainstem. Neurons here take information from other cells all over the body. Such nuclei have various functions, and are distinguished by names drawn from Latin. Nuclei are like a modem being wired to a home internet network. Any information reaches the router from your cable connection or telephone line, the information is stored in the router, and other information is then sent out from the router to your device, TV, and any other devices linked to your network.

There are two main types of neurons and in one of two ways, they send information. The first are afferent neurons that receive information about what's happening inside and around the body. Afferent neurons take information toward the brain from the body, called afferent memory. The second is called efferent neurons, which send information to various organs and structures throughout the body with regulatory or motor effects (called efferent information), so that efferent information is transported from the brain to the body.

The vagus nerve is attached within the brainstem to four separate nuclei. Eighty percent of the information that the VN transmits is afferent information, meaning that the most common direction that information flows in the VN is from the body's organs to the brain. The remaining 20 percent of VN neurons have an efferent signal, spreading from the brain to the body, contributing to specific functions in each cell and organ. It's interesting to hear that most medical students are surprised by the fact that only 20 percent of the VN's work is efferent, as it has so many efferent effects on the organs—just think then how much information this nerve relays back to the brain, more than four times as much as the information it relays away from it.

Like the wires of your home network connection, the bundles of neurons within your nerves send information along their length using electrical signals that result in the release of a chemical signal called a neurotransmitter upon reaching the end of the nerve. Such neurotransmitters bind to receptors on the receiving cells, resulting in the cells at the end of the contact having an effect. The major neurotransmitter used by the VN is called acetylcholine (in short, ACh), which has a significant anti-inflammatory effect in the body.

Managing the inflammatory system is one of the VN's most important functions; it is the body's major inflammatory control system, and has far-reaching effects on your personal health and illness.

Inflammation is a major reaction within the body to keep us safe from bacterial and viral pathogens, physical trauma and other things that should not enter the body optimally. The results can be wide-ranging and contribute to many different health problems when inflammation rates are not kept in check and become chronic. Certain common conditions correlated with high levels of inflammation include:

- Alzheimer's disease
- Arthritis
- Asthma
- Cancer
- Crohn's disease
- Diabetes
- Heart and cardiovascular disease
- High blood pressure
- High cholesterol
- Postural orthostatic tachycardia syndrome (POTS)
- Ulcerative colitis
- As well as any condition that ends in the suffix –itis

Most of the organs impacted under these circumstances become internalized (or connected) through the VN. It is therefore not only possible but highly likely that the VN works sub-optimally and does not have its anti-inflammatory effect on these organs, leading to chronic inflammation and illness.

It is important to remember that these conditions do not occur in isolation and if there is one of these conditions, it is likely that there will be another. The same signals are sent to and from virtually every internal organ via the vagus nerve, so if inflammatory rates are not regulated in one organ, the same is likely to occur in other regions.

FASCINATING FACTS ABOUT THE VAGUS NERVE

1. The vagus nerve prevents inflammation.

It is normal to have a certain amount of inflammation following injury or illness. But there is a link between overabundance and many illnesses and disorders, from sepsis to autoimmune rheumatoid arthritis. The vagus nerve runs a vast network of fibers around all the organs positioned like spies. When it detects a signal for the incipient inflammation— the presence of cytokines or a substance called tumor necrosis factor (TNF) — it warns the brain and activates anti-inflammatory neurotransmitters that control the immune response of the body.

2. It helps you make memories.

The study of rats at the University of Virginia found that activating their vagus nerves strengthened their memory. The activity released the norepinephrine neurotransmitter into the amygdala which preserved memories. Related trials have been conducted in humans which propose possible therapies for disorders such as Alzheimer's disease.

3. It helps you breathe.

Induced by the vagus nerve, the neurotransmitter acetylcholine tells your lungs to breathe. It's one of the reasons why Botox — often used cosmetically — can be potentially dangerous, as it interrupts your production of acetylcholine. Nevertheless, you can also activate the vagus nerve by taking abdominal respiration or holding your breath for four to eight counts.

4. It's intimately involved with your heart.

In the right atrium, where acetylcholine release slows the pulse, the vagus nerve is responsible for controlling the heart rate via electrical impulses to specialized muscle tissue— the heart's natural pacemaker. Physicians will calculate your heart rate variation, or HRV, by calculating the time between your individual heartbeats, and then plotting this overtime on a graph. These data can provide clues about your heart and vagus nerve resilience.

5. It initiates your body's relaxation response.

The vagus nerve advises the body to calm out by releasing acetylcholine as the ever-vigilant sympathetic nervous system revives the fighting or flight responses—pouring the stress hormone cortisol and adrenaline into your body. The tendrils of the vagus nerve stretch to many tissues, functioning as fiber-optic cables that give instructions for releasing enzymes and proteins such as prolactin, vasopressin, and oxytocin, which calm you down. People with a stronger response to the vagus may be more likely to recover faster after stress, injury or illness.

6. It translates between your gut and your brain.

The heart uses the vagus nerve as a walkie-talkie to tell the brain how you feel by "action potentials" electrical impulses. Your gut feelings are very real.

7. Overstimulation of the vagus nerve is the most common cause of fainting.

When you shudder at the sight of blood or whilst you get a flu shot, you are not frail. Your body, responding to stress, overstimulates the vagus nerve, causing your blood pressure and heart rate to drop. Blood flow is limited to your brain through intense syncope, and you're losing consciousness. But most of the time, for the symptoms to subside, you simply have to sit down or lie down.

8. Electrical stimulation of the vagus nerve reduces inflammation and may inhibit it altogether.

Neurosurgeon Kevin Tracey was the first to demonstrate vagus nerve stimulation would significantly reduce inflammation. Results on rats have been so good he has repeated the human experiment with amazing results. For rheumatoid arthritis — which has no known cure and is often treated with poisonous drugs— hemorrhagic shock, and other equally serious inflammatory syndromes, the invention of implants to activate the vagus nerve by electronic devices shows a drastic reduction, and even recovery.

9. **Vagus nerve stimulation has created a new field of medicine.**

Spurred on by the success of vagal nerve stimulation to treat inflammation and epilepsy, the medicine's future may be a burgeoning field of medical study, known as bioelectronics. Using electrodes that transmit electrical impulses to different parts of the body, scientists and doctors are aiming to treat disease with less drugs and less side effects.

CHAPTER 2

WHERE IS THE VAGUS NERVE LOCATED?

The longest nerve in the body is the vagus nerve. Without becoming too complicated, let's look at where the nerve starts and how it moves and enters the organs it innervates and sends information from and to. Let's go through the body along its course.

BRAINSTEM CONNECTIONS

In the brainstem the neurons that form the vagus nerve begin, coming from four separate nuclei. Such nuclei are formed by the dorsal motor nucleus, the solitary nucleus, the spinal trigeminal nucleus and the uncertain nucleus. Each of these nuclei regulates nerve fibers unique to their components.

Sensory nerves carry signals from the skin that the spinal trigeminal nucleus is innervated by the vagus nerve. It involves a specific section of the ear's tissue, which is necessary when using acupuncture therapy to stimulate the vagus nerve and will be discussed in later chapters. Signals from the body's internal organs are carried via the vagus nerve to the solitary nucleus and moved up into the brain for further processing. Such signs include stomach, intestine, kidneys, pulse, kidney, gallbladder, pancreas, and spleen. We can also send direct signals through the vagus nerve to these organs using parasympathetic fibers which originate in the dorsal motor nucleus. Such impulses help to calm and control the heart and lungs activity, and improve the stomach and digestive tract, kidney, pancreas, gallbladder, and spleen action.

The nucleus ambiguus is the final nucleus which contributes fibers to the VN. This nucleus sends out motor acting neurons, primarily working to regulate certain muscles found in the throat and upper airways. Such muscles are responsible for keeping the airway open and transmitting sound through the vocal cords, thus generating the voice.

The right and left vagus are the only nerves in the body that have four different functions and four distinct nuclei contributing specifically to component fibers. Most other body nerves deliver basic sensory information to the muscles from the skin, and motor impulses for movement. This simple distinction should make you aware of the true importance of the vagus nerve, and the wide scope of its function.

INTO THE NECK

The fibers of the left and right vagus nerves reach into the cranial cavity (the inside of the skull) from the brainstem area known as the medulla oblongata and fuse to form what we call the vagus nerve. The nerve then travels through an opening from the skull called the jugular foramen. This hole represents a large gap between the neck and the brain for the nerve and other blood vessels to move. Once the VN leaves the brain, between the inner jugular vein and the central carotid artery, it enters the upper neck area just behind the jaw. Such blood vessels are the main bloodlines from and to the brain and are highly important to keep us healthy.

Being so close to these individual blood vessels is an indicator of how vital the vagus nerve is, because physical damage to any of these three components will cause irreparable damage. In the case of the blood vessels, damage can lead directly to death while nerve damage will result in a complete lack of function in many body organs.

Immediately after the jugular foramen passes through the vagus is a thickening of the nerve called the superior ganglion (or jugular ganglion). A ganglion is a thickening of a nerve that is created by a group of sensory cell neuron bodies located very close to each other. In this ganglion, the cell bodies of the sensory nerves congregate and then organize into the thinner nerve segment, which forms the first division of the vagus nerve.

The VN's first branch is known as the auricular branch. The auricular branch travels through a gap called the mastoid canaliculus back into the brain, and through another skull hole called the tympanomastoid fissure toward the jaw. The nerve stretches out towards each ear's surface. This branch detects pressure, temperature, and wetness on the ear skin; in particular, the outer canal, tragus, and auricle. Auricular acupuncture (acupuncture points in the ear) is the main target for induction treatment of VN dysfunction.

As the nerve continues to pass down (or inferiorly, using anatomical language) from the upper ganglion, the VN thickens again to form the lower ganglion, also known as the nodose ganglion. The ganglion houses the neuronal cell bodies involved in bringing in input from the internal organs. The nerve then thins out again and enters a passageway formed by a thickening of the connective tissue called the carotid sheath immediately. As it travels through the heart, the vagus nerve, together with the internal carotid artery and the internal jugular vein, is given extra soft tissue protection.

The vagus nerve sends us their next branch within the carotid sheath: the pharyngeal branch. The pharyngeal branch includes vagus nerve neurons but also bears some supplying neurons (glossopharyngeal and peripheral nerves) from the ninth and eleventh cranial nerves. Once these neurons merge, they move over to the body's midline before they reach the upper portion of the mouth, called the pharynx. The vagus nerve in the pharynx relays motor impulses to various muscles involved in the swallowing reflex, controls the opening and closing of the upper airway and regulates the gag reflex.

This gives rise to the third branch, known as the superior laryngeal nerve, as the vagus nerve descends the sides of the neck within the carotid sheath. This nerve branches off the VN very soon after the pharyngeal node, and provides motor signals to the larynx muscles above the vocal cords, precisely the muscles that regulate the voice's pitch.

As the VN runs down through the carotid sheath, it gives rise to the branches of the cervical cardiac, which are two of the three branches that instill the muscle. Shortly after leaving the carotid sheath in the chest (thorax) region the third branch, the thoracic cardiac branch, emerges. Such branches intermingle with the nerves of the sympathetic nervous system and form the cardiac plexus (a plexus, pluralized as plexi, is a series of intermingling nerve fibers of various branches and separate nerves of origin that migrate towards a specific location). We have two cardiac plexi: one is called the shallow cardiac plexus in front of the aorta, and one is called the deep cardiac plexus behind the aorta's arch. (The aorta is the principal blood vessel carrying blood from the heart to the rest of the body.)

Many cardiac plexi fibers stretch to the heart's sinoatrial (SA) node, while others travel to the atrioventricular (AV) node. In the next part, we will address the role of those nerves on the heart. The most important thing to remember for now is that these fibers regulate the electrical activity rate that drives the blood.

INTO THE THORAX

This runs down into the thorax, behind the first and second ribs, and in front of the wider blood vessels that stretch from the heart, after the nerve leaves the bottom of the sheath.

The left vagus nerve crosses the aorta's arch before (anterior to) and then sets off its fourth branch— the intermittent laryngeal nerve. The right vagus nerve follows a similar path on the opposite side of the body; however, it passes in front of the right subclavian artery and then sends off its fourth branch, the recurrent laryngeal nerve on the right side.

Both recurrent nerves of the laryngeal follow a similar path, but on opposite sides. These are the nerve's only roots that are moving and heading upward again towards the heart. Based on tensioning and loosening of the vocal cords, they bring motor signals from the brainstem to each of the larynx muscles below the vocal cords, which are essential for vocal sound production. We're going to discuss more about how we can use those specific branches to help improve the vagus nerve if it works suboptimally.

Once the nerves enter the aorta level, each of the vagus nerves sends branches off to the next set of organs, the lungs. The left vagus nerve sends a pulmonary branch to the anterior pulmonary plexus, and a pulmonary branch is sent to the posterior pulmonary plexus by the right vagus nerve. These branches of the nerves mix with sympathetic neurons, reorganize and then travel to each side to innerve the lungs. These branches go to the bronchi and larger branches of the lungs to open and close them on the basis of each situation according to the body's needs.

One organ in the thorax which is often extremely neglected or ignored by the vagus nerve innervates: the thymus. The thymus is an immune system's extremely important organ. It is found in the chest's mediastinum, just before the heart but behind the sternum. A vagus branch makes its way to that nerve to carry out messages to and from the thymus. The thymus is the primary source of preparation for and production of our white blood cells early in our life. The reason this organ is so easily forgotten is because it shrinks over time and is replaced by fat tissue. The process starts during childhood, and can go on into early adulthood for many years. Think of thymus as a school for young immune cells, and as the school gets older and deteriorates, the consistency of the preparation that the white blood cells go through drops.

INTO THE ABDOMEN

The last segment the vagus nerve innervates is the gastrointestinal organs. These organs are important for nutrition, for controlling the immune system, and for ensuring that the blood that enters the rest of our cells does not contain toxins that can adversely affect cell health.

The vagus nerve's first abdominal branch goes out into the stomach. Once our body is in the rest-and-digest stage, the vagus nerve fibers activate the activity of the stomach muscles. They send signals to the parietal cells to produce and secrete hydrochloric acid (HCI), the main cells to produce and secrete the pepsin and gastrin digestive enzymes, and the smooth stomach muscle cells to actively churn and transfer the food in our stomach into the next digestive tract, the small intestine.

If the vagus nerve is weakened and these essential impulses are not sent to the stomach cells, it will lead to problems like hypochlorhydria, or poor stomach acid, which is a major root cause of many health conditions. To activate the digestive enzymes and break down food, sufficiently low pH (high acid) is needed. The maximum stomach pH level should be around 3.0 in the uterus, while nothing above 5.0 will be high enough to cause pepsin and gastrin. High stomach acid allows for less efficient digestion of food. Low pH in the stomach can also make it possible for harmful bacteria, viruses and parasites to penetrate the intestines and cause havoc on your digestive tract.

The vagus' second intestinal segment heads into the liver. Ironically, these divisions are closely associated with the sense of hunger and the need for certain forms of nutrients. First the food we eat comes into the stomach to be broken down. It then continues into the small intestine, where most of our macronutrients (fats, sugars, and protein amino acids) are processed into the bloodstream. These nutrients then flow into the liver for filtration, processing and sending back to the brain via the portal vein.

From the heart, the vagus relays information about blood sugar levels, fat intake and general activity of the liver to the brain. The vagus nerve can also relay information about the amount of bile required to assist in the digestion of fats. The liver has many functions that include vagus supply, including and certainly not limited to the processing of bile and bile salts (the active component of bile), which are then sent to the gallbladder for storage; the balance of blood sugar by generating glucose; the control of hunger and satiety by calculating fat intake; the filtration of blood in the portal vein that contains all nutrients; To our general well-being the liver is very necessary and the vagus innervation is strongly associated with keeping this equilibrium.

The gallbladder is closely connected to the stomach. The gallbladder is often ignored by the medical system, which is necessary for our bodies to function optimally. When the liver produces bile and bile salts, they are sent for preservation into the gallbladder in preparation for the next meal. The gallbladder pumps bile into the duodenum (the small intestine's first part) to help bring fats into the bloodstream when the next meal happens. The gallbladder pump is mediated by the nerve of the vagus. The vagus branches off from the liver to send messages to the gallbladder, activating the smooth muscle cells in its walls to pump bile into the digestive tract. It arises in response to a meal decided by the taste buds (sensory receptors on the tongue) containing fat, which should be digested once it enters the small intestines.

The next branch of the vagus is to the pancreas. Your pancreas is one of the most vital glands in your body, having both an exocrine and an endocrine component. The endocrine pancreas directly produces and secretes insulin and glucagon into the bloodstream to regulate blood glucose (blood sugar) levels. The exocrine pancreas stimulates and secretes digestive enzymes directly into the small intestine through a channel. The three most important digestive enzymes produced by the pancreas are protease, which breaks down proteins into their amino acid components; lipase, which breaks down fats into free fatty acids and cholesterol from their components; and amylase, which breaks down carbohydrates into simpler sugars.

Vagus innervation sends signals back into the brainstem from the pancreas, relaying information about the state of exocrine and endocrine cells. It also relays information about food intake from the brainstem back to the organ and what enzymes are needed for production and release into the bloodstream and digestive tract. Vagus innervation is important to transmit this information, as a lack of signaling can hinder the release of digestive enzymes, reducing the effectiveness of the digestive process.

Once the vagus nerve travels past the stomach, it forms the celiac plexus, a network formed between sympathetic lumbar nerves and vagus parasympathetic fibers. This network sends branches to the rest of the abdomen's organs.

The spleen is the first organ which is innervated after the celiac plexus. The spleen is located opposite the liver on the left side of your body, below the left lung. The purpose is to track the bloodstream and activate or deactivate immune system cells depending on what they are sensing. All spleen and thymus control immune cell activity early in our lives, but later in life after the thymus has vanished this role is regulated by spleen alone.

The spleen receives signals from the sympathetic branches to activate the inflammatory pathways that arise in response to or injury from physical and biochemical traumas. The parasympathetic branches send signals to interrupt the mechanisms of inflammation. The vagus nerve modulates a system called the anti-inflammatory cholinergic pathway, which has significant effects in spleen.

After the celiac plexus the next branch of the vagus passes to the small intestine. Once the chemical and physical churning in the stomach has broken down food it enters the small intestine. Here the pancreatic digestive enzymes and bile undergo more digestive fermentation. The small intestine has the function of breaking down and absorbing most of our macronutrients. These include fats, sugars, and proteins (which typically break down into their amino acid components). The bloodstream receives the macronutrients the small intestine's lining cells have accepted.

The bite of food we take (which at this stage in the digestive process is called chyme) must be moved along the length of the small intestine twisting and coursing. To this effect, the vagus nerve stimulates the digestive tract's smooth muscle cells by signaling the extensive network of nerves lining the intestine, called the enteric nervous system.

We have an immensely important interaction within our digestive tracts with the other cells. I am concerned about the symbiotic relationship between our human cells and the microbes that live in our intestines: our microbiota. Within our large intestine, the bigger, narrower region of the digestive tract, the vast majority of our bacterial allies live. While many essential vitamins, nutrients and biochemical precursors are produced for us by these bacteria, they can also generate other toxins and methane. We need a system that can keep these bacteria in check and relay the digestive tract and microbiome function status signals to our brain. Thus, while the vagus nerve activates smooth muscle cells to push food along the rest of the digestive tract, the microbiome's main relay path to talk to the brain is also. The vagus nerve inwardly travels around the first half of the large intestine— the descending and transverse parts.

The final organ that the vagus nerve innervates is actually two organs, with one on each side of the body— the kidneys. These organs have a couple of different functions crucial to our health. In the form of urine, the kidneys pump fluid out of the bloodstream, a mixture of uric acid and water, which is then sent back to the bladder. The vagus nerve is a major controller of kidney function, and thus has a major role to play in controlling blood pressure.

The vagus nerve does not actually stop at the close of its course. Instead, it forms a final plexus from the lower end of the spinal cord with the parasympathetic nerves of are. Such parasympathetic fibers innerve the second half of the large intestine, which is called the descending and sigmoid colon, as well as the kidney and sex organs.

CHAPTER 3

THE FUNCTIONS OF THE VAGUS NERVE

An optimally working VN is absolutely paramount when it comes to improving wellbeing and preventing disease progression. There are many explanations for this and in this chapter we'll go through some of them.

One body that functions optimally is like a symphony orchestra. Each of the various instruments has specific parts to play in a symphony, and optimal harmony can only be achieved if each instrument is directed toward doing its job. The orchestra's conductor manages to ensure that no instrument is off-tune or tempo, as a single error could lead to terrible performance. A conductor that does not keep its end up will also result in a broken performance.

The vagus nerve is the conductor of a symphony orchestra for the human body. It controls the activity of so many different organs and cells in our body, but only when it functions optimally can it do so. The body's multiple organs and cells must be capable of detecting and communicating correctly. Dysfunctional signaling can result in a loss of equilibrium in the system, and ultimately a disorder and disease state.

Let's break down all of the various functions the human body orchestra conductor performs— the vagus nerve.

- **Sensing Skin of the Ear**

The first branch of the vagus nerve, as discussed in the previous chapter, is the auricular branch, which is directly involved in feeling the skin of the ear's auricle, tragus, and external auditory canal.

This branch's function is pure in sensation, allowing us to feel pressure, touch, temperature, and moisture on each ear's central section. This is clinically relevant and quite significant, as this is one of the major areas where the VN can be activated using therapies such as acupuncture.

- **Allowing Food to Be Swallowed**

The last thing you think about when you eat a meal is the process of swallowing every bite and pausing the breathing reflex so you don't choke. The vagus nerve copes with this important task.

The second branch of the VN (the pharyngeal branch) regulates the activation of five pharynx muscles: the three constrictor muscles at the back of the throat and two other muscles that link the throat and the soft palate (the soft tissue at the back of the mouth's roof). Such muscles are involved in the pharyngeal process of swallowing which includes moving the chewed food towards the larynx and the esophagus while holding it out of the trachea, thereby keeping the airways free of food. The active motor part of the gag reflex is also regulated by this VN branch.

This is clinically important, as poor vagus nerve function will lead to coughing and a change in gag reflex function. This meditation can be used to better balance the VN with constructive movements to stimulate the gag reflex.

- **Managing Your Airway and Vocal Chords**

Are you conscious of the effort required to keep your upper airways open with every breath you take? The muscles involved in that process are also involved in your voice development. If you have ever wondered what nerve is responsible for ensuring verbal communication with those around you is feasible, that's the vagus!

Superior and frequent laryngeal nerves are the third and fourth branches of the VN. The muscles above the vocal cords are responsible for the superior laryngeal branch while the recurring laryngeal branch is responsible for the muscles below the cords.

The superior branch of the laryngeal carries motor information to some larynx muscles and controls vocal pitch. Suboptimal feature of the superior branch of the laryngeal results in a pitch transition. A chronically hoarse voice or an easily fatigued, monotonous voice in this branch of the nerve is a sign of poor vagal tone (signaling capacity). Irritation of this nerve can also lead to severe cough and the risk of aspiration (i.e., food or drink entering the trachea by impaired vocal cord function).

The recurrent laryngeal branch carries motor information to the muscles below the vocal cords, allowing the vocal cord structures to form sounds by opening, closing and tensioning. It also has a sensory component which relays information of these structures from the esophagus, trachea, and internal mucous membranes. Dysfunction of these nerves during physical activity contributes to heaviness, speech loss and trouble breathing.

Those laryngeal muscles control the airway's opening, closure and working. Hence, any coughing or speech problems can be due to reduced activity and sound of the vagus nerve. Airway respiration and muscle tone are of supreme importance for vagal control. Any persistent obstructions to a safe and well-functioning airway will impede the function and signaling signals from these muscles, which will affect the vagus nerve flow adversely.

- **Controlling Breathing**

What about taking a breath? Okay, the vagus also has a role to play in managing this vital function. The VN's pulmonary branch runs into the pulmonary plexus, connects to the sympathetic nervous system, and innervates both lungs' trachea and bronchi. The vagus component is a sensory nerve that relays information about lung expansion levels to the brain, as well as the levels of oxygen and carbon dioxide.

In the lungs the activation of the vagus nerve slows the respiration rate and deepens the breath. Breathing appears to be slower during the rest-and-digest process, and comes from the diaphragm rather than the breathing aid muscles, and the breath rate tends to be lower. A slow, deep breath rate will activate the vagus nerve and stimulate the relaxation reflex when a person is transitioning from a combat-or-flight state into a rest-and-digest phase.

Vagus tone is expected in the pharynx, larynx, and trachea to open the airway. The pharynx and larynx muscles are innervated by the VN motor components. These neurons ' suboptimal activity can lead to obstruction of the airways, as occurs in chronic obstructive pulmonary disease (COPD) and obstructive sleep apnea. Both of these symptoms are a sign of low vagal tone and an activation of the vagus nerve.

- **Controlling Heart Rate**

Your heart beats to get blood filled with carbohydrates and oxygen into each of your tissues, and to take toxins to the organs that can dispose of them. The VN plays an important role in ensuring heart rate stays within a comfortable range when the body is not under threat. Without the VN, our heart would not be working close to its optimum pace.

The vagus nerve is connected directly to the sinoatrial node, which sends electrical signals to the two atria (the thinner chambers at the top of the core). It is also connected directly to the atrioventricular node which manages the ventricles' pumping rate and contraction pressure (the two thicker, lower chambers of the heart).

The sympathetic nervous system activates the heart during fight-or-flight times to increase the pumping rate and the pressure of the contractions in both ventricles. After the stressor passes, the rest-and-digest phase takes over, and the body moves towards a phase of vagal activation. At this time the VN's parasympathetic fibers slow the heart rate and actively lower the pumping contractions pressure. These fibers work to lower heart activity, allowing the heart to rest and recover from stressful times and severe activation.

- **Maintaining Optimal Blood Pressure**

Blood pressure is an important determinant of the amount of fluid in the bloodstream. The kidneys function to filter out the body's fluid and toxins and are thus the major manager of blood pressure in the body. The vagus nerve relays information from and to the kidneys to help it control the flow of water and urine from within the kidney glomeruli, the kidney's essential filtration unit, while controlling the body's internal blood pressure. When the body is under stress, through the vagus and sympathetic nerves, signals from the blood vessels (in particular the carotid body) are relayed up the brainstem and back down to the kidneys. The kidneys then restrict their blood vessels and increase blood pressure by reducing the amount of water from the bloodstream being filtered out. When the body is calm, carotid body impulses instruct the kidneys to pump out more water and dilute the blood vessels to relieve blood pressure.

Hormones, interacting with the vagus and sympathetic nerves, are also intimately linked to this cycle. The immediate control therefore comes from the nerves and the hormones dictate the sluggish, steady management.

High blood pressure is a normal condition and medications are often used to regulate these levels. High blood pressure can be a symptom of overactivation of the stress hormones of the adrenal glands and the stress response of the sympathetic nerves. It is also a very common sign of damaged vagus nerve and poor vagal tone.

- **Controlling the Many Functions of the Liver**

The vagus nerve relays substantial information from and to the brain, handling its almost 500 functions.

The liver controls where blood flows within the body. When the body shifts into fight-or-flight mode during times of stress, blood flow is pushed towards the arms and legs to increase muscle activation and allow us to fight off an attack or run away from it. Blood flow in the liver should decline, because feeding and blood filtration are not a priority for survival during this stressful event. When the body is calm and at rest-digest, the activation of the vagus nerve decreases and the blood flow to the liver increases. During these times, priority is given to feeding, blood filtration, and other cellular flourishing functions.

The vagus nerve also controls the liver cells that produce bile and bile salts, as well as transporting bile into the gallbladder and small intestine. It has been shown that these cells, called cholangiocytes, are active when the vagus nerve is active, and increase bile flow to the gallbladder for storage.

Bile performs multiple liver and body functions. Through a two-step process, the liver detoxifies fat-soluble toxins, creating a water-soluble waste product to be released. Bile contains certain toxins that are made harmless and ready to be discharged from the body by our feces through the digestive tract. Stool is just one of three routes for removing the waste products. Some waste disposal forms are as saliva through the liver, or as sweat through the skin.

Bile salts, the bile's effective constituent, have another role to play. When bile is released into the small intestine, waste product and ball salts are released. The bile salts are needed to escort triglycerides (fat molecules) from the digestive tract, through the enterocytes (cells lining the small intestine), and into the bloodstream. Fats cannot be absorbed without being escorted by bile salts, which is a bad thing because fats and cholesterol have many vital functions within the body. That also results in fatty stools. In this function, the role of the vagus nerve is to activate cholangiocytes and to open the flow of bile from the liver into the gallbladder and from the gallbladder into the small intestine so that enterocytes can absorb fat.

- **Activating Gall Bladder Emptying**

Once the liver produces bile and the cholangiocytes send that bile into the gallbladder, it is stored and matures, like a fine wine, until it is necessary. When eating a meal, the taste buds in the tongue and the rest of the mouth give signals to the brain, letting our body know about the macronutrients it tastes as part of every bite and the whole of the snack or meal. If the central nervous system suggests that fats are being ingested then the vagus nerve will quickly signal that bile will be required for the liver and gallbladder.

After receiving this signal, the gallbladder stimulates the smooth muscle cells in its lining and pumps the bile out into the small intestine through the bile duct to aid in the absorption of food. The gallbladder will remain full without this vagus nerve signal, and will not drain out the requisite bile— a condition known as obstructive cholestasis.

The removal of the gallbladder, called cholecystectomy, is one of the most common procedures taking place in hospitals and clinics in north America. Obstructive surgery to remove a gallbladder, such as gallstones, is often the first option given to patients who start experiencing pain associated with obstructive cholestasis. Unfortunately, most patients don't get the chance to determine the root cause of this condition.

Gallstones are a painful issue which may affect the gallbladder. After a long period of low vagus nerve function, gallstones form in the gallbladder which would prevent the gallbladder from adequately pumping out bile and bile salts. If bile salts stay long in the gallbladder, they start crystallizing and forming blocks. It tends to occur with a lack of activation of the vagus nerve and is an early sign of weakness in that nerve. In clinical settings it has been shown that gallstones may be released in early cases of this condition when the vagus nerve starts to function at a higher level.

- **Managing Hunger and Satiety**

Satiety is attained when our brain receives vagus nerve signals. We require signals from the liver to be satiated, indicating we have enough fat, protein and carbohydrates in the body. Both carbohydrates and fats are metabolised in the liver.

The following control is mediated by the vagus nerve in terms of carbohydrate metabolism: When blood sugar levels gradually decrease, afferent vagal fibers in the liver increase activity and signal to the brain that more carbohydrates are required by the liver cells. Nevertheless, this mechanism does not signal abrupt changes in blood sugar; these are detected immediately within the brain.

The small intestine releases a hormone called glucagon-like peptide 1 (GLP-1) as a response to increased levels of blood sugar which the body translates as satiety. Diminishing levels of GLP-1 signal the vagus nerve, which in turn manages a slow reduction of blood sugar. Many pharmaceutical companies are now producing medicines that work along the GLP-1 pathway to help manage hunger; however, activating the vagus nerve can manage this within your own body.

The vagus nerve provides yet another road to satiety sensations. After eating a meal, vagal afferent neurons transmit information to the brain about the amount of fats, particularly triglycerides and linoleic acid, that have made their way to the liver. This activates the function of the vagus nerve and sends a signal to the brain which produces a feeling of satiety and a desire to stop eating.

An underactive vagus nerve may not be able to send the signal efficiently, resulting in constant feelings of hunger, loss of satiety, and overeating at mealtime. After a meal it will take less than 15 to 20 minutes to feel full when the VN is working effectively. If you know someone who lacks the feeling of satiety, and their hunger persists even after a big meal, they probably suffer from VN dysfunction.

- **Managing Blood Sugar and Insulin Levels**

Insulin resistance and levels of type II diabetes are on the rise at exorbitant rates. Obesity and properly called diabesity—concurrent diabetes and obesity — are big signs of a lifestyle that is unhealthy. Weight problems and problems with blood sugar control are big signs that something in your body is working sub-optimally.

Our bodies shift their balance towards the sympathetic nervous system during times of stress and release more of the adrenal stress hormones, specifically cortisol. Cortisol's primary effect is to increase blood sugar by stimulating a process called gluconeogenesis, which is when new glucose is created from fat and protein stored in the hepatic system.

In short bursts it is necessary to use the sympathetic nervous system to keep us alive and to allow us to survive. This fight-or-flight mechanism developed in response to potential survival threats — think of our ancestors running away from a sabre-toothed tiger. In this situation, when our bodies have to shift to survival mode when the stressor approaches us. We either have to combat the threat, or take the flight and escape as quickly as possible.

Our skeletal muscles require significant energy-forming resources to facilitate the fight-or-flight response— preferably, the fastest-acting and most easily accessible way to form cellular energy that would allow us to survive the threat. Our bodies can generate glucose rapidly, use gluconeogenesis for short-term fuel to transfer it through the bloodstream. The sympathetic nervous system swiftly shifts blood flow to the arms and leg muscles to make us extra strong and fast, while shifting it away from the digestive tract and kidneys. We can then easily use our bodies to fight the threat or to sprint away as quickly and humanly as possible.

The concern with this method is that it is often more aggressive than is absolutely necessary for longer periods. Under the chronic stress that we face at work and at home, with our jobs, marriages, friends, and relatives, and because of metabolic stressors and covert diseases, our bodies tend to stay in the fight-or-flight mode significantly longer than they should, and we don't shift back to the rest-and-digest state in which the parasympathetic recovery system is predominantly involved. The inability to shift back causes the liver to produce glucose continuously, which in the longer term leads to higher levels of blood sugar. The pancreas is activated to form insulin in response to the high blood sugar levels. Insulin is the messenger that indicates to each of our cells that they take glucose from the blood and use it to make energy.

- **Managing the Release of Digestive Enzymes from the Pancreas**

Not only is the pancreas involved in the control of blood sugar; it is also highly responsible for producing and secreting digestive enzymes in the small intestine in response to a meal.

When we eat, our small intestine taste buds and sensory cells send signals to the brain that determine the specific macronutrients present in the meal. Is it protein, fat and/or starch in the meal? How much of the digestive tract has reached each, and how fast? Once the answers to these questions are determined, the vagus signal the pancreas to release specific digestive enzymes — proteases, lipases, and amylases — to assist in the breakdown of these macronutrients, allowing our cells to digest these nutrients and eventually use them properly.

In response to higher protein levels, the pancreas secretes proteases to help break down the bonds between the amino acids that make up the proteins. The pancreas secretes lipases in response to higher levels of fats, to help break down triglycerides into cholesterol and free fatty acids. Finally, amylase is secreted to help split complex carbohydrates into simple sugars in response to higher levels of carbohydrates.

Without this process, the important macronutrients required for cellular function would not be absorbed by our bodies. Amino acids are mostly involved in creating new proteins for intracellular signalling within our cells, including protein and peptide hormones, neurotransmitters, receptors and certain enzymes. The free fatty acids and simple sugars are used mainly for energy generation, while the cholesterol component of the fats is used as a precursor to steroid hormones such as estrogen, testosterone and cortisol. All of these molecules are important for cellular function so an optimally functioning pancreas is essential to ensure that these molecules make it into the bloodstream.

- **Managing Gut Motor Function**

It is an important role of the vagus to get food from the mouth to the opposite end of the digestive tract. We chew that food down in our mouth after taking a bite of food until it is physically able to be swallowed and transported through the rest of the digestive tract.

Once that food, or bolus, hits the back of the mouth— the pharynx — it's the vagus nerve's job to push it into the next area. The sensors and muscles lining the digestive tract must function properly for this to happen. As each bite hits the back of the throat, a stretch reflex in the smooth muscles is elicited, which alerts the brainstem through the vagus nerve, letting it know where the bolus is. Its addition, the VN is signaling the smooth muscle cells for engaging its motor action and moving the food bolus downward. That process is called peristalsis.

In fact, this seemingly simple function is very complex and necessary since the digestive tract is quite long. We are required to move along the digestive tract to extract nutrition from our food and push out any unwanted visitors.

A poorly toned VN may be a root cause of an impaired bolus movement through the tract. Chronic constipation and diarrhea are undoubtedly signs of poor vagal tone and lack of muscle and nerve activation. Some of the main problems that cause this issue are that we don't chew our food well enough, and that we eat in a hurry and too hard. This is what I call the drive-through effect, as we eat in a rush while in a stress-filled environment. We are attempting to trigger a rest-and-digest cycle while in a state of fight-or-flight.

For now it is necessary to understand that nourishment can move along this path— from the pharynx to the esophagus, through the stomach, into all three parts of the small intestine, and against gravity in the ascending and transverse colon — without a properly functioning vagus nerve.

- **Managing the Activity of the Immune System**

Think of this question: Would you be driving a car with no functioning brakes? A car has the important function of moving you safely from point A to point B and the important function of your immune system is to keep you safe from attacking cells and proteins. And just as a car needs a system of checks and balances, like brakes, so your body's immune cells need a similar set of checks and balances.

The immune system can run amok without its brakes and start attacking human cells, which can lead to autoimmunity, or even stop attacking tumor cells which can lead to cancer. A car can be a very hazardous tool, without brakes. The immune system can also be quite risky, without a system to keep it in check.

Overview of the Immune System

The Body's defensive system is the immune system. It protects you from invaders and unwanted toxins that can lead to unfavorable health conditions, and often do so. This system includes white blood cells which send out sensors to search for body invaders. We roam through the bloodstream in an optimally working environment, identifying proteins and pathogens that have invaded the body and sending signals to other immune cells whose role is to remove such invaders which should not be present.

In the immune system, there are multiple types of white blood cells, commonly classified as leukocytes, namely monocytes, macrophages, neutrophils, mast cells, and dendritic cells, collectively known as phagocytes; as well as basophils, eosinophils, lymphocytes (T cells and B cells), and natural killer cells.

"Phagocytes" simply means "cells that feed." Once they detect dead or dying human cells, harmful bacteria and unsafe proteins that should not be there, they activate and literally start engulfing the unwanted cells or proteins, initiating a process called phagocytosis. They break down these invaders and create debris in the immune organs and liver, which is later filtered out of the blood. Each phagocyte senses various invaders and has a different way of breaking them down, but all of these cells are essential for an effective and balanced immune system that works.

As well as phagocytosis, mast cells are also highly involved in allergy and anaphylaxis, as they absorb and release histamine-rich granules. Those are likely to be hyperactive in a person with similar reactions and chronic allergies. Mast cells are seen to be highly active in autoimmunity, by ensuring we experience the symptoms of the condition. Also, they are one of the only immune cells in both the gut and the brain. If mast cells become over-activated within the brain, the brain's nerves may become more sensitive to pain, leading to inflammation of the brain. Likewise, when these cells become stimulated in the stomach, they make the gut's nerves more responsive to pain, contributing to swelling of the gut around the nerves, which will hinder the normal movement of the gut (peristalsis) motility.

Basophils are responsible for inflammatory responses during an immune response, and are active in diseases such as mast cells that cause allergic symptoms such as anaphylaxis, asthma, atopic dermatitis, and hay fever. Parasites and allergies can trigger them. Both of these can commonly occur and enter the body through the digestive tract or broken skin.

Eosinophils are responsible for responding to parasites and infections and for fighting them. We are also considered, as basophiles, to be active in allergies and asthma. Low-grade, chronic parasite or bacterial infections can cause overstimulation of eosinophils, which have been shown to trigger asthmatic and allergic symptoms. Such diseases most usually affect us and get through our bodies through the digestive tract.

The main cells involved in suppressing infections and tumor growth in the body are programmed killer cells. They do not need sensors to identify human cells as opposed to invading cells, hence the name of natural killers. Dysfunction of these cells can lead to tumor growth and the body's ability to identify and combat these cancerous growths may decrease.

The vast majority of leukocytes generate sensors which roam the body's internal environment to do their job. These sensors are called immunoglobulins, or anticorps. Such sensors come in five different types— immunoglobulin A (IgA), IgE, IgG, IgM, and IgD.

Each of these sensors has a different role and speed, at which the white blood cells are signaled to react.

IgG is the most abundant sensor and is found on mature immune cell surfaces. Their function is to recognize non-present cells and proteins, and to activate a pathway which leads to inflammation and immune activation.

IgA is the second most plentiful receptor and a particular type of IgA (called secretory IgA) is sent to our body fluids such as breast milk, saliva, and digestive tract secretions. Secretory IgA is important for identifying potential threats, like mouth, to the digestive tract. High levels of IgA indicate the presence of bacteria, viruses, parasites and yeast while low levels of IgA indicate dysfunction of the immune system due to chronic activation by these same invaders. In my patients I test secretory IgA levels to assess their current immune response and activation status. This is a very important and useful instrument used in the practice of functional medicine.

They are far less common in IgM, IgE, and IgD. They are located on the surface of adult immune cells, and have a function similar to IgG.

The system is mediated through the vagus nerve to keep immune cells in check. An essential mechanism called the cholinergic anti-inflammatory pathway is required to set off a properly functioning vagus nerve. The pathway keeps the immune system in balance when involved, and pumps the brakes when appropriate. Vagus innervation to the digestive system, such as thymus, spleen, and intestines, is heavily involved in stimulating the process. It's important to learn how these important organs work within the immune system before you learn about the pathway itself.

The primary lymphatic organ is the thymus. It produces predominantly T-cells, white blood cells which seek and destroy foreign invaders. To activate it, the vagus nerve sends a branch to the thymus, while it may be deactivated by sympathetic fibers that connect to this organ. The thymus on average is fully functional until we hit puberty, when it starts to shrink and decrease in both size and function. This process is referred to as "thymus involution." Recent research has shown that our high-stress lifestyle and sympathetic branch hyperactivation can lead to earlier thymus deactivation. This is assumed to be a root cause of autoimmune conditions and an increased risk of bacteria, viruses and other invaders becoming infected.

The immune systems have been learning and growing earlier in the lives to create a system that helps to protect us from invasion by bacteria, viruses and other pathogens that should not enter our bodies. This is a dynamic system, one that takes years of training and preparation to deal with the body's invaders. Overstimulation of the thymus may occur through parasympathetic fibers and may result in excessive organ growth; however, this is not very common. The far more common problem is that there is a higher level of sympathetic activation, which actually prematurely deactivates the organ.

So long as you have a thymus that functions well the body is covered as it grows. The thymus functions as a classroom, or immune cell training facility, the body's police officers. It continues to pump out fully qualified and highly intelligent police officers who protect our cells from invaders as long as this training facility is active and fully funded. When the funding for this school drops, fewer, less well-trained officers are released, and the level of protection withers, putting us at a much higher risk of invaders infection.

This shows why we are at a higher risk of infectious disease as we grow older and also why we are at a higher risk of autoimmune conditions following highly stressful events in life. Our immune cells are not equally suited to distinguishing invading cells from our own cells in an autoimmune condition. When we age, we are subjected to stressful life circumstances, thereby increasing rates of autoimmune conditions, including, but not limited to, thyroiditis of Hashimoto, rheumatoid arthritis, multiple sclerosis, Crohn's disease, ulcerative colitis, and many more.

The spleen is the next checkpoint for immune system cells. Speak of spleen as the White and Red blood cell buffer. It ensures there are only qualified, fully trained immune cells in the body's bloodstream and other tissues. It will remove and filter out any cells which approach the end of their optimum operating period. The spleen acts as a check and balance for circulation immune cells. This means that the immune system guards from pathogens while functioning optimally while not behaving aggressively against our own cells. The vagus nerve relays back and forth information between the central nervous system to let our bodies know which cells are drained out of the blood.

Like the thymus and so many other organs, the parasympathetic activity of the vagus is necessary to keep the spleen active while the sympathetic activity temporarily decreases or shuts down splenic activity. Chronic stress or activation of sympathetic branches will undoubtedly lead to consistently lower levels of spleen activity and in addition to inadequate filtration of white and red blood cells. This leads to a higher likelihood of autoimmune disease, as the less trained roaming "police officers" are not kept in check and can not differentiate between strangers and our own cellular proteins.

The immune cells nearest to the region determine the danger and produce proteins called cytokines to recruit more cells that will assist in the immune response when a harmful event occurs in the body or when threats are identified. Such cytokines are produced by afferent fibers of the vagus nerve, which send signals back to the brain to warn it of the level of inflammation that is occurring. Recent research has even shown that cytokines may be identified by the vagus nerve.

The intestine is the most common area where invaders can enter the body, and as such, the vast majority of our immune cells are located in the gut lining. Throughout the digestive tract they are held in small pockets which we affectionately refer to as gut-associated lymphoid tissue (GALT). The functions of the vagus nerve in the intestine are quite extensive and necessary to guarantee optimal health. It helps to regulate immune and inflammatory responses, encourage us to create memories and relay information between the bacteria in the gut and the brain.

- **Managing Inflammation in the Gut**

Through this mechanism, the vagus nerve uses the neurotransmitter acetylcholine (ACh) to send signals to the cells of the immune system throughout the body but especially strong signals in the gut. These impulses are designed to soothe immune response and reduce inflammation.

Afferent vagus activity in the thymus and spleen has been shown to increase in response to stressors like lipopolysaccharide (LPS), a toxin that is created and released by one of two types of bacteria, and invaders such as microbes, viruses and parasites in our gut. At the same time, the nervous system's protective branch, the fight-or-flight reflex, makes sure immune cells are able to attack the attackers. Once immune cells first detect the presence of these unwanted stressors in the intestine, they send a signal to the GALT which activates a stress response and the sympathetic nerves. The sympathetic nerves then signal the norepinephrine neurotransmitter (NE), also called adrenaline. NE activates the cells of the immune system which are highly reactive to invaders and stressors. This system is extremely effective, but brakes are required for optimal operation, as with all important systems.

Parasympathetic activity is carried on through the vagus nerve in the vast majority of the heart. The role is to regulate inflammation and immune response. To counteract the pro-inflammatory response of sympathetic nerves and norepinephrine, the vagus nerve and its branches send out ACh in the gut and other areas of the body. The perfect balance between sympathetic NE secretion and parasympathetic ACh secretion occurs when working optimally. It holds our health in balance by triggering an immune response as needed and shutting it off if it is not needed. Command of a feature comes from turning it off.

In response to higher levels of stress and immune activity ACh is released from the vagus nerve. The release is significantly and efficiently intensified by the enteric nervous system, a group of nerve cells in the gut which is so huge, it is also known as the second brain. Some argue that the enteric nervous system in our head is more important than the brain, because the interaction between this system and our microbiome dictates much of our health.

The effect of ACh on immune cells is facilitated by an important receptor found on the surface of most white blood cells— the alpha-7 nicotinic acetylcholine receptor. This receptor works to lower activation and slow down the immune response when it is not needed. The parasympathetic and sympathetic activation of inflammatory response in the gut is crucial in balancing.

- **Allowing Us to Create Memories**

Recent research has shown that gut bacteria are essential for the growth and maturation of both the enteric nervous system and the central nervous system. When described above, the vagus nerve is heavily involved in relaying microbial information from the intestinal bacteria to the brain. This communication chain could be responsible for activating the production of a protein called neurotrophic factor (BDNF) derived from the brain. BDNF activation leads to increased neuronal connectivity, and most importantly, to memory production in the brain.

That means it can be difficult to form new memories and create new neuronal connections without gut bacteria and a healthy functioning vagus nerve. To an even greater degree, this means that if you have an optimally functioning vagus nerve, you are likely to be able to form larger memories and associations with the world around you and those that matter to you.

We are creating defenses during our fetal development to shield us from external threats. One such barrier is the gut-blood barrier which protects us from bacteria (both good and bad) that may want to invade. It is made from the same cells that create our barrier to the blood-brain. This ensures that any infection that happens in the stomach and breaks down the intestinal barrier also has the ability to break down the blood-brain barrier.

Ever walked into a room, and forgot why you went into that room? Have you ever tried to say something quite simple but couldn't find the right words to say? These problems are commonly referred to as brain fog, and are caused by higher than optimal levels of inflammation in the brain. Brain fog happens when the blood-brain barrier has partially broken down, and toxic impulses may enter the brain tissue, thereby reducing neuronal activity.

Brain fog shows the presence of inflammation in the brain caused by a blood-brain barrier that is less than optimal, and therefore poorly functioning gut lining or leaky intestines.

CHAPTER 4

EXERCISES FOR ACTIVATING THE VAGUS NERVE

Only when we have a well-functioning ventral branch of the vagus nerve will we reach optimal health. The activities and strategies in this section will help most people move from either chronic sympathetic spinal chain activity (stress) or dorsal vagal activity (shutdown) to a social involvement state. Such techniques can also be used to discourage creation of disorders within the autonomic nervous system, and to preserve a general level of well-being.

When you begin to do these exercises for the first time, it is advised that you start a simple journal. Write down any signs or complaints that may be bothering you.

Note how often a particular symptom has shown up. For starters, the condition might appear "all the time," "every morning," "once a week," or "once a month." If you have regular migraine headaches, the aim is definitely to be completely free of migraines; nevertheless, any progress would be accepted as a positive outcome.

Note the strength of your symptoms. You may write "They annoy me, but I get through the day regardless," "They allow me to take medication," "They're so intense I can't go to work or take part in normal social activity," "I can't sleep," or "I can't get out of bed in the morning." You may choose to assess the pain or discomfort using a scale from one to ten.

After doing the workouts, you can look back at your chart and note the changes— for example, "The migraines are less regular," "The discomfort is less intense," or "I spend less money on painkillers every month." Think on how the exercises helped— that you don't have the symptoms so often, or that the condition isn't so severe. Any signs remain may be fading or vanishing as you continue to do the workouts.

You might also note other positive changes—do you sleep better, for example? Better breath? Is your stomach getting normaler? These all lead to improved health and resiliency.

The Basic Exercise

The goal of this exercise is to increase social interaction. This replaces the atlas (C1, the first cervical / neck vertebra) and the axis (C2), which improves stability in the neck and spine as a whole. (See "Axis" and "Atlas" in the Appendix) This increases blood flow to the brainstem from which the five cranial nerves required for social engagement derive. This can positively affect the ventral branch of the vagus nerve (CN X), as well as the cranial nerves V, VII, IX and XI.

Simple, easy to learn, and easy to do, the simple exercise takes less than two minutes to complete.

BEFORE AND AFTER DOING THE BASIC EXERCISE

Evaluate your head and neck freedom of movement. Rotate your head to the right as comfortable as possible. Turn to the middle then stop and tilt the head to the left. How far are you going to move towards each side? Is there any discomfort, or rigidity?

Make those same movements again after doing the workout. Is there any difference in your range of motion? If you had pain when you were turning your back, did the movement minimize the pain level?

BASIC EXERCISE INSTRUCTIONS

The first few days that you are doing the routine you will lay on your back. After you are familiar with the exercise, you can do it sitting on a chair, lying on your back or standing.

- Lying peacefully on your stomach, linking one hand's fingers together with the other hand's fingers
- Put your hands behind the back of your head, the weight of your head resting comfortably on your interwoven fingers. With your fingertips you can feel the hardness of your cranium, and feel the muscles of your feet on the back

of your head. If you have a sore shoulder and can't get both of your hands up behind the back of your head, it's enough to use one hand, with the fingertips and palm coming into contact with both sides of your head.
- Keep your head in place, look right, just lift your eyes to the degree you can. Do not turn your head; just keep your eyes going. Glance to the extreme.
- You'll cough, blink, or breathe after a short period of time—up to thirty or even sixty seconds. This is an indication that your autonomic nervous system has relaxed. (A typical inbreath accompanies an outburst but a sigh is different—after you breathe in, a second inbreath comes on top of the first inbreath before the outbreath.)
- Take your eyes back to look straight ahead.
- Put your hands in place, and hold your head straight. Turn your head to the left this time
- Keep your eyes there until you hear a smile, a yawn or a slur.

Now that you've done the Basic Exercise, take off your hands and sit or stand up.

Evaluate what you've been through. Has your neck's mobility got any improvement? Did it change your breathing? See anything else?

THE NEURO-FASCIAL RELEASE TECHNIQUE

The Basic Exercise is a simple self-help method, and an easy and effective way of achieving better ventral vagus nerve function. But, if you're a body trainer, you might want to use your own hands instead of doing workouts with people; or you might want to mix the self-help exercises with hands-on strategies.

The procedure of neuro-fascial release will act as an alternative to the Basic Exercise. It is particularly valuable for handling autism spectrum infants, children and adults who lack the necessary verbal communication abilities to receive guidance on the simple exercise when it may be difficult to communicate with them and have them obey the orders. Using your hands like that allows you a nonverbal way to bring about beneficial changes in the nervous system of another human.

NEURO-FASCIAL RELEASE TECHNIQUE INSTRUCTIONS

If you're used to doing acupuncture, you'll need to use your hands in a new way to make this procedure a success. Practice this method on your own and learn how to get a break before using it on somebody else. To bring about social engagement with this procedure, reflexes in the nerves in the loose connective tissue just below the skin above the base of the skull need to be activated. It regulates the stress levels in the small muscles between the base of the skull and the neck vertebrae.

Understanding this technique will be better if the person lies on his or her back, so you can see the fingers clearly. Start with one side of his head's back.

- Gently push the base of the skull to one hand, and note the occipital bone's stiffness. Check one side of the occiput for the skin's "slide-ability." Slide the skin softly onto the bone to the right. Then let it revert to neutrality.
- Then slide the skin to the left, and let it get neutral again. There was more opposition in what direction?
- Slip the skin into greater resistance. Go very slowly and at the very first sign of resistance be ready to stop. It may have just shifted one-eighth of an inch or less. Hold on, and hold that position. Keep feeling the slightest opposition. The person will yawn or swallow in the gap when you're not doing anything and the tension in the skin will melt away as it escapes.
- The skin will slip quickly in both directions until you check it again.
- On the other side, replicate procedure.

This should work properly when you check the vagus nerve again. Further freedom of movement should also be practiced by turning the head left and right.

TWO-HANDED NEURO-FASCIAL RELEASE TECHNIQUE INSTRUCTIONS

You can use 2 hands once you've trained using one hand.

- Place one hand finger on one side of the occiput at the base of the back of the head. Check the skin's slide-ability over the bone. The skin should more easily slide over the bone in one direction than in the other.
- Place a finger at the top of the neck on the same side of the other hand. If you're going a little harder you can feel the muscles. Use this finger to check the skin's slide-ability over the muscles at the tip of your spine. It should move in the opposite direction more easily that the other finger slides over the bone of the skull
- Lighten your pressure after you have tested it. Let your two-handed fingertips move the skin in opposite directions before you encounter resistance.
- Hold tight, hold on to that mild tension; wait until you get a breath or drink.
- Close the fingertips, and return the skin to its original position.

- Do the same thing on the head, on the skull and neck opposite side.

If you are testing the vagus nerve again, it should work properly now. Further freedom of movement should also be given when moving the head to the left and the right.

PROPER APPLICATION OF THE NEURO-FASCIAL RELEASE TECHNIQUE

The key to success with the technique of Neuro-Fascial Release is to slide the skin and stop at the first sign of resistance. Using the lightest touch possible, use your fingers to communicate with your skin. Slide the skin over the internal layers of muscles, bones, and tendons a very short distance instead.

This approach varies from the methods used in other types of mas-sage, primarily targeting the muscle structure and thus moving the body into it. Take the time to read the notes step-by-step so that you can learn how to do it properly.

This hands-on procedure spreads the damaged connective tissue just below the skin itself. This connective tissue is rich in ends of the proprioceptive nerves. You establish a little friction in this loose tissue, which is enough to relax certain nerves, as you softly move the skin over the muscles and bones a very short distance.

You slide the skin only a short distance, until you feel the very first sign of resistance, and because you work directly on the proprioceptive nerves you don't have to use the force required by most muscle-focusing forms of massage. If you use unnecessary force and keep pushing after the first sign of resistance, or if you move the skin too quickly, it will potentially contract the muscles and ligaments. This way, you can't cause any damage— release only takes longer. You may not get the desired changes, at worst.

You may find that you push so lightly at times that the other person reports that they can't feel anything at all. That would be a good feedback!

As you progress with the treatment, you will notice tangible improvement in the skin's slide-ability.

THE SALAMANDER EXERCISES

The following "Salamander Exercises" are gradually increasing flexibility in the thoracic spine, freeing up movement between the individual ribs and the sternum in the joints. This will increase your breathing capacity, help reduce a forward head posture by getting your head back into better alignment, and reduce scoliosis (abnormal spine curvature).

Eighty percent of the vagus nerve fibers are afferent (sensory) fibers, meaning they bring back information from the body to the brain, while only 20 percent are efferent (motor) fibers which carry instructions from the brain to the body. Some of the afferent fibers from CN IX and CN X sections monitor the amount of oxygen and carbon dioxide found in the blood. By improving our breathing pattern with these exercises, we're telling the brain (via afferent nerves) that we're safe and our visceral organs are working properly. This in turn encourages development in the ventral vagus.

But what come first? Is a reduced breathing pattern the product of a dysfunctional ventral vagus, or is input from a less than adequate breathing pattern caused by a lack of ventral vagus function? If there are ten-sions in the pulmonary diaphragm and the muscles that shift the ribs, input from the afferent vagal nerves controlling such movements can indicate irregular breathing, which can avoid a state of ventral vagal action, just as restoring ventral vagal activity will boost the physiological condition; in fact, either one is beneficial, regardless of which occurred first.

A forward head position reduces the amount of space available to breathe in the upper chest. The Salamander Exercises can create more space for both the heart and the lungs in the upper chest. Reducing a forward-head stance will also relieve friction from the nerves that enter the heart, lungs and digestive organs from the spinal cord. The Salamander Exercises can relieve pressure on vertebral arteries by strengthening the positioning of the cervical vertebrae, and can reduce certain back pains between the arms.

You raise your brain to the same level as the rest of your body, when you do the Salamander Exercises. This pose is similar to that of a salamander who does not have a tail, so that at the tip of the spine his head is like an additional vertebra. A salamander cannot stretch, extend, twist, or side-bend his head independently in relation to the spine's first vertebra, or lift his head above the spinal vertebra point, as reptiles and mammals can. This exercise is done in line with the spine, with the head.

Such exercises put your head in a position that is neither up nor down in terms of your spinal movements. The thoracic (the chest part of the spine) is now more able to bend horizontally, somewhat like a salamander. In your thoracic vertebrae, you may use side-bending motions to relieve muscle tension between your ribs and the thoracic spine. It makes the lungs move freely and encourages healthy breathing.

There is typically greater flexibility in the neck and lumbar vertebrae in the expansion and flexion of the human spine, and less flexibility in the thoracic spine. However with side-bending, the thoracic spine's strength increases dramatically. The thoracic vertebrae facet joints are opened, making for a more free side-bend of the thoracic spine.

LEVEL 1: THE HALF-SALAMANDER EXERCISE

To do the Salamander exercise first part to the right, sit or stand in a comfortable position.

- Makes your eyes look to the right without turning your head.
- Continue to face forward, turn your head to the right so that your right ear moves closer to your right shoulder without raising your shoulder to meet it
- Hold your head thirty to sixty seconds in this position.
- Then let your mind get neutral again, and change your eyes to look forward again.
- On the other hand, do the same now: let your eyes look to the left, then tilt your head to the left. Return your head to an upright position after thirty to sixty seconds, and your eyes towards a forward target.

THE HALF-SALAMANDER—A VARIATION

Follow the same instructions above in this variant on the Half-Salamander exercise but let your eyes look to the right when turning your head to the left. When you move your head this turning of your eyes in the opposite direction increases your range of motion; you should be able to bend your head even further to the side. Hold this for thirty to sixty seconds, then turn back on the other side to do the same thing.

LEVEL 2: THE FULL SALAMANDER EXERCISE

The movement on Full Salamander includes side-bending the entire spine rather than just the neck. They use another body position, too.

- Get down on all fours, protecting your knees and hand palms with your weight. You can rest your hands on the floor, but it's better if you put your hand palms on a desktop, table, chair seat, or sofa pillows. Your eyes should be on the same plane as your neck
- In this exercise, your ears should not be raised above your spine or lowered below that point. Lift your head slightly above what you think is right, in order to find the right head position. You should be able to feel the head is raised slightly. Then, slightly lower your head under what you think is right. You should know like the head is below what it should be. In between the two positions go back and forth. Put a little of your head up and take it down a little. Try to find a halfway place where the head doesn't move too far up or down. Even though you might never immediately reach the spot, you will start to zero in on it.

- Once you have found a good head position relative to your back, look right with your eyes, keep them in that position, and turn your head sideways to the right by turning your right ear towards your right shoulder.
- Complete the turn by allowing the curve in your side to extend past your jaw, all the way down to your backbone.
- Hold this position for 30 to 60 seconds.
- Put the spine back to the center.
- Repeat all above steps, but on the left.

FINDING AND DEFUSING TENSION IN TRIGGER POINTS

When you operate on nerves on the muscle surface, a light touch is usually enough to relieve the tension in the muscle as a whole. Rather than massaging the whole body, as is usually the case for ordinary massage, merely massaging the trigger points is appropriate. You don't have to work hard, or press the body deeply.

Massaging trigger points thoroughly or with a great deal of pressure is usually painful, and can be detrimental. The body does not feel safe under excessive pressure and the autonomic nervous system is placed in a state of sympathetic activation or withdrawal of the dorsal vagus. This isn't detrimental, but it's unsuccessful because it takes the body time to settle down.

Make some small circles on the point of the trigger. Then stop and wait before you detect a yawn or a slur in the form of a nervous system reaction. The severity of the pain will continue rising or fading within a few minutes. If migraine relief is required, you can repeat the procedure.

Not all the X's need to be viewed on painting. Even if an X shows a trigger point for a specific pain pattern, if you don't feel something rough or unpleasant at that particular spot on the muscle surface, the trigger point is not involved. Don't waste time trying to release it, but focus on the triggers that feel tough, thick, or painful.

SCM EXERCISE FOR A STIFF NECK

This exercise will extend your range of motion as you rotate your head, relieve stiff neck symptoms and help prevent migraine headaches. It's similar to the very first moves we made as infants lying on our stomachs, supported on our elbows, with our heads free to move in order to look around.

- Lie down on your butt. Head up, and put your arms under your chin. Support your upper body weight on your knees
- Rotate your head to the right as far as you can safely go. Hold the position for 60 seconds.
- Return your eyes to the middle.
- Now rotate your head as far as you can comfortably go, and hold that position for 60 seconds.

When, with this exercise, you have increased the rotation of the head but the mobility is still not as strong as you want it to be on one leg, then the constraint probably comes from another muscle, the levator scapulae, which is inerved by the spinal nerves C3–C5. The only way to eliminate this kind of stiff neck is by strengthening the work of CN XI and the trapezius and sternocleidomastoid muscles.

Twist and Turn Exercise for the Trapezius

The Twist and Turn exercise enhances the tone of a flaccid muscle trapezius, balancing each of its three parts with the other two. It also helps lengthen the back, improve movement, and proper head alignment (FHP) in the forward. This in turn also ease pain in the shoulder and back.

This activity has the potential to benefit everyone, not just those with FHP. It takes less than a minute to make it, and the feeling of positive change is overwhelming. It's a good idea to take a minute to do this workout whenever you're stuck for a while, and repeat it from time to time periodically.

The concept behind this movement is not to reinforce the trapezius muscle, nor to stretch it. The belief is that the muscle is strong enough to flaccid muscle fibers and just need nerve stimulation. You wake them up and take on their share of the work, just like they did when we were kids and walked on all fours.

When a baby lays on its back, it uses all the muscles of the trapezius muscle's three parts to hold the roots of the shoulder upright, raise the chin, and tilt the head to look about. The baby later also uses all these muscle fibers to crawl and look around when he raises himself up on all fours.

When an infant stands up, however, the trapezius fibers are not used equally any more. Some become more nervous, while the energy goes out of other fibers to flaccidise. Each three sections of the trapezius muscle no longer supports the brain in the same way. With time, the head begins to float further forward, so the bases of the hands are in front of the shoulders ' center. The shoulders then show a propensity towards the midline to move forward and downward.

You'll get a more even tone in all the muscle fibers of the three sections of your trapezius after doing this workout. Instead, when you're standing or sitting, your head simply glides back and up by itself, rising FHP and strengthening your balance.

TWIST AND TURN EXERCISE INSTRUCTIONS

The exercise has three parts. The difference between your arms is the position of the three parts.

- Sit comfortably on a firm surface, like a chair seat or a bench seat. Keeping the eyes ahead.
- Fold and cross your shoulders, your palms gently leaning on your elbows. You'll move your shoulder girdle briskly, first to one side and then to the other side, without slowing and without moving your hips.
- Let your elbows drop in for the first part of the exercise and rest just in front of your body. Rotate your arms and transfer your wrists, first on one leg and then then on the other. The muscles float gently around the chest as you move your head from side to side. It stimulates the upper trapezoid fibres.
- Have it completed three times. Do not strain, and do not halt movement. Do not push or squeeze the shoulders; your movements are quick and calm.
- The second part is the same as the first one; the only difference is that you raise your elbows and keep them in front of your eyes, at heart level. Then move the elbows to one side and then to the other side. Do this quad. It stimulates middle trapezius muscle fibers.
- Lift your elbows as far as you can safely, and replicate the above movement for the third part. Rotate the knees, three times from side to side. This activates your lower trapezoid muscle fibers.

You may find after you've finished the exercise that your head feels lighter and has rotated back and up, away from the forward-headed pose. For someone with considerable FHP, it's not unusual to become an inch or two taller the first time they do the workout. If someone comes at you from the side, if you have that habit, she will see that your head has moved back slightly from its initial forward position.

A FOUR-MINUTE NATURAL FACELIFT, PART 1

The benefits of this gentle and friendly therapy include calming the facial muscles and strengthening the role of cranial nerves V and VII, leaving a more natural smile in place. You can do this on your own, and share it with others. This exercise:

- Improves the movement of your skin
- Lives in the middle third of your face's speech muscles, in the region between the corners of your mouth and the corners of your eyes
- Improves blood circulation in your face's skin
- Brings a vibrant appearance of liveliness that you can sense and others can see
- Helps you smile more easily and more often
- Makes your face more sensitive to interactions with others, and thereby increases your sense of empathy
- Makes flat cheekbones a little more prominent and makes very high cheeks a little flatter.

Look into your face in a mirror before you do this procedure. Give him a hand-held mirror when you're doing the procedure on someone else so he can watch his expression and monitor the adjustments. Look particularly to the skin area around the cheekbones.

First do on one side of the face. Then test if the two sides can see or sense a difference. When you talk or smile, the differences are usually obvious. Then do the opposite side. Also, there should be more symmetry.

WHERE TO DO THE TECHNIQUE

There is a spot on the face which is the endpoint of the meridian of Large Intestine acupuncture, called LI 20. In Chinese, Japanese, and Thai massage, it's a beauty point. This point is called "Golden Bamboo" in Classical Thai Massage. This point is called "Welcoming Fragrance" in Traditional Chinese Medicine, and it clears the nostrils, increasing the breathing.

In terms of Western anatomy, this stage in Chinese medicine is interesting. It lies directly above a joint between two facial bones, the maxilla and the premaxilla. In the evolutionary development of our genus, the two bones were separate entities long ago, but at an early stage they calcified together into one single bone. The maxilla / pre-maxilla is just one bone in western anatomy, or the maxilla.

The source is easy to find of the Broad Intestine meridian. Just raise the skin gently about an eighth of an inch to the top side of the supra-alar crease (the bend between the cheek and the upper lip), close to the outer edge of the nostril. When you explore the area with your finger, you'll easily find this point because it's more sensitive than the rest of the skin around.

HOW AND WHY TO DO THE TECHNIQUE

Branches of the fifth cranial nerve innervate the surface of the facial skin. Touching your face's skin gently activates the nerve endings.

- Brush the skin surface with a very light contact at acupuncture point LI 20. Then let the fingers melt along with the flesh.
- Move the skin upwards and downwards to figure out which direction is more resistant. Move the tension gently. Arrange.
- Hang on, and wait to see it released.
- Slide the skin inwards towards the midline of the face, and outwards towards the side to find a more resistant direction.

- Hang tight, just drive gently. Keep the button, and wait.

The facial muscles are innervated by seventh cranial nerve (VII) branches. Just below the skin are two layers of facial muscles.

- At the same level, let your fingertip sink softly into the layers of muscle beneath the skin. Let your fingertip stick to the first muscle pad, as if it were Velcro.
- If you're careful not to push too hard, and if you feel what's going on beneath your fingertips, you can slide these muscle layers; first slide one layer over the other, making a small circle.
- When you walk around the circle you can find more resistance to skin slipping in one direction. Continue to push gently in that direction, and stay until a sigh or swallow release happens.
- And press forward gently. Now the lower muscle layer remains along with the top muscle layer and fat. All layers can be rolled together over the bone base.
- When you step around the circle you can find more resistance to skin slipping in one direction. Continue to push gently in that direction, and stay until a sigh or swallow release happens.

All bones are bound by a connective-tissue called a periosteum (peri-means "about" and osteum means "bone." The tissue is very rich in spinal nerve endings, or, in this case, cranial nerves.

- Let your fingers dig into the face ever further until you rest gently on the bone sheet.
- Massage on the periosteal surface has a profound effect on the autonomic nervous system. Press lightly, but hard enough for Large Intestine 20 to reach the bone surface. Let your fingertip on the surface of the bone move from side to side, then hold a light pressure on the bone, and wait until a release is made.

This bone had been two bones in the embryo, the maxilla and the pre-maxilla. Although these have merged into one bone, it is still possible for most people to feel like two different bones existed previously.

This cranial nerve massage V and VII stimulates the skin nerves and the face muscles. It does not remove all the wrinkles, but it relaxes the facial muscles, reduces some lines and helps the face look healthier and more polished. And there are no negative side effects or scar tissue from a facelift treatment or harmful Botox accumulations.

Most specifically, this treatment makes the face become more vocal, more communicative and more responsive — more socially active. The expression should be versatile and capable of communicating different emotional responses in different situations. Facial expressions are an essential part of our communication with others.

Facial versatility is important not only for communicating our own emotions but also for social engagement. If our face is relaxed when we look at the face of another, our own face automatically makes micro-movements that mimic the facial expression of the other. Such gestures are very low, and rapidly alter.

Through the afferent pathways of cranial nerves V and VII, these changes in tension in our skin and facial muscles then feed back into the brain, giving us immediate subconscious information about what others feel. That is a prerequisite for us to have another person's empathy.

In general, when facial muscles under the skin are relaxed, a person usually has a smooth, friendly and what is seen as a beautiful or attractive face. Unfortunately many people have been trapped for years in the same mental and facial pattern. Their facial muscles tug on the skin, forming a double chin or wrinkle. If the person remains in the same emotional state and does not relax his or her facial muscles, these wrinkles will become more profound over time.

A gentle brush of the skin of the face activates CN V in relation to this procedure, which decreases stress in all facial muscles.

A FOUR-MINUTE NATURAL FACELIFT, PART 2

Part 1 focuses on LI20, an acupuncture point on the side of the nostril to the Large Intestine meridian. Stimulating this aspect improves the flexibility and toning of the lower face muscles around the mouth and nose. Its effect, Part 2, concentrates on the head. In many ways, the actual technique is similar to the first face-lifting technique you did on Large Intestine 20. On the inside corner of the ear you'll note acupuncture point B2. Apparently, people sometimes brush this idea off when they are sleepy, without worrying about it. Massaging facial skin and muscles here is often self-reassuring.

Link to B2 by using the thumb or one finger. At B2, work your way down either layer: the fat, two muscle layers and the periosteum.

This point is also a trigger point for the muscle of the orbicularis oculi, a long, smooth muscle that encircles the eye opening. The eyes are sometimes called the soul's mirror. The muscle might be too rigid when we operate on B2, leaving the eye slightly closed or it might be undertoned, leaving the eye open too. Once we finish, the balance between looking outwards and looking in will be strengthened. You will see another person more plainly, and it will be easier for this person to make eye contact with you and perceive you differently.

This acupuncture point is, at a deeper level, at the tip of a small facial bone called the lacrimal bone. The word "lacrimal" means crying. A person's eyes can sometimes be cold and seem dead. Through rubbing this bone at B2 and keeping your contact onto the lacrimal bone, you can regulate the influx of moisture to your eyes and keep them warm and shiny. Facelifting massage's goal is to leave a smile on your lips, and a twinkle in your eyes.

- Look for a more receptive location at the inner corner of the eyebrow than the surrounding areas.
- Use your fingertips first to lightly brush the skin a few times.
- Put your fingertips on the skin slightly at point B2 (see above) and keep the touch with the skin's surface until you get a sigh or swallow release.
- First, gently press back into the facial muscle sheet. This is where the muscle of the flat, circular orbicularis oculi, which runs around the jaw, connects to the face bones. Let the skin adhere to your finger and make a small circle, moving the skin gently, looking for the direction in which resistance is present.
- Keep your finger on that resistor until a breath or swallow release happens.
- Then go deeper, until you feel the bone's surface. Rub that up a couple times.
- Keep the bone in contact, then wait for a release.

If the muscle of the orbicularis oculi is too hard to shut the eyelids into a squint, then this should open the eye more naturally. If the eye is too wide-open, this technique should make it somewhat firm but leave it still open.

This is the second of two Classical Thai Massage beauty spots.

VAGUS NERVE YOGA

A vagus nerve yoga practice aims to become more flexible... not of the physical body but of the nervous system. Evidence has shown enormous yoga effects for improved vagal tone, decreased stress and recovery from trauma. This will make you become more able to switch between compassionate and parasympathetic nervous system more quickly and with greater choice. The following 7 vagus nerve yoga practices will help you develop a safe vagal tone, stimulate as needed, relax as desired and regain balance in your life:

- **Conscious Breathing:** The most effective way to change the equilibrium between sympathetic and parasympathetic behavior on the nervous system is through breathing. Vagus nerve yoga focuses on diaphragmatic breathing and extending the exhale length to counterbalance any over-stimulation of the sympathetic nervous system. Research has found that slow, diaphragmatic, rhythmic breathing increases healthy vagal tone. One type of yogic breathing is Ujjayi pranayama which, by engaging your whisper muscles, causes a slight constriction in the back of your throat. To learn this breath, exhale as if you were fogging up a mirror from your mouth. Then, breathe the same way just shut the mouth and exhale out of the nose. You will hear the deeper sound of your breath that often sounds like ocean waves. Start with an even count for inhalation and exhale. As with the inhalation, slowly increase the length of your exhale for even greater relief. You might begin with a4-count on the inhale for example and exhale the exhale to a 6 or 8 count exhale. That will calm your parasympathetic nervous system.

- **Half-Smile:** Engaging in a "half-smile" is a valuable way of changing your mental state and cultivating a feeling of serenity right now. Because the vagus nerve reaches into the face muscles, you can raise the vagal tone by relaxing the face muscles and then turning your lips slightly upwards. This practice helps activate what Dr. Stephen Porges calls the most advanced branch of the vagus nerve, the "internal nervous system." Imagine your jaw softening as you smile, and a relaxed feeling spreading across your face, all your head and down your shoulders. Notice the subtle contextual shifts in your thoughts and emotions.

- **Open your Heart:** With yoga postures which open across your chest and throat, you can gently stimulate the vagus nerve. Consider this simple sitting exercise of opening your heart by raising your hands to your feet. Inhale as you stretch over your arms, extend your elbows wide, and raise your chin. Exhale in front of your heart as you pinch your wrists, then tuck your chin. In this moving meditation take a few deep breaths. Focusing on the inhalation can be calming and uplifting in this breath pattern. Let yourself stretch into the open heart.

- **Wake up and Stretch:** If you're having a hard time waking up in the morning or feeling tired and sluggish in the afternoon yoga can provide a gentle pick me up for your mind and body. Practice standing postures such a warrior stance (virabhadrasana) to revitalize your mind and wake your body up. Notice your feet-to-earth connection to remain grounded to energize yourself in a balanced manner. Allow the breath to remain rhythmic, so you remain rooted and connected to your body's sensations.

- **Release the Belly:** You will deal with the vagus nerve connection as it traverses the abdomen. Enter a table position with your hands under your shoulders and your knees under your hips. If your knees have any pain you should bring a folded cushion under you. When you inhale, start lifting your head and shoulders toward the stage, dropping your belly when you step into Cow Pose. Drop your head and shoulders on your exhale, thus raising your back into Cat Pose. Use your own rhythm with your breath for the dance. Repeat as many times as you like, creating a gentle stomach and spine massage for you.

- **Self-Compassion or "Loving Kindness" Meditation:** Self-compassion and the "loving kindness" tradition are encouraging you to indulge in the act of friendliness towards yourself and others. Research on those individuals who practice a meditation of loving kindness revealed increased vagal tone, increased autonomic flexibility, increased sense of social connection and more positive emotions. Take a moment to consider an obstacle that you face in your life. Imagine another facing a similar challenge now. Would you evoke a sense of empathy or sympathy towards this other person? Note how the body experiences this sensation of love. Wish them good. See if you can add to yourself that same level of affectionate kindness? Wishing you back.

- **Yoga Nidra**: Restorative yoga can help slow down your nervous system and calm it down. Another classic practice is Yoga Nidra, also referred to as "yogic night" or a peaceful meditation. Yoga Nidra is the solution to our chaotic, modern lifestyle and by stimulating the parasympathetic nervous system, it offers the opportunity to heal body and mind. Cultivate body consciousness and breath until you reach a comfortable spot lying on the floor, pillow or yoga mat. Make room for anything you feel including any areas of tension, heaviness, or constriction. Let yourself stay still for 30 minutes to enjoy a deeply relaxing and nourishing experience.

FACTORS THAT HELP STIMULATE THE VAGUS NERVE

1) Cold

According to one study on 10 healthy people, the fight-or-flight (sympathetic) response reduces when the body adjusts to cold temperatures, and your rest-and-digest (parasympathetic) system improves, which is regulated by the vagus nerve. In this analysis, cold temperatures were known as 50 ° F (10 ° C).

Sudden exposure to cold (39 °F/4 ° C) also increases activation of the vagus nerves in rats.

Despite not having observed the influence of cold showers on vagus nerve sound, many people advocate for this traditional method of cooling.

Before the advent of water-heating techniques all showers were cold showers when we think about it. Anecdotally, cold tubs are popular in Japan, while many Northern nations participate in ocean dips during the winter or early spring for special occasions.

Nonetheless, becoming used to completely cold showers usually takes a while. Some people say it is good to start by dipping your face in cold water.

However, remember to consult with your healthcare provider first. For people with heart disease or those at risk, most doctors recommend cold showers against them. That's because sudden exposure to cold can restrict the blood vessels, which can increase heart rate and blood pressure.

2) Singing or Chanting

Singing raises the Heart Rate Variability (HRV) according to one interesting study on healthy 18-year-olds.

The variation in heart rate has been correlated with recovery, enhanced stress tolerance and adaptation, and decreased rest-and-digest (parasympathetic) behavior.

The writers of the above study found that chanting, mantra singing, hymn singing, and upbeat positive singing all improve HRV in subtly various ways.

They hypothesized singing would initiate a vagal pump's work, sending relaxing waves through the chorus.

Singing at the "top of your lungs" might also manipulate the muscles in the back of your throat to stimulate the vagus.

The authors of this study, on the other hand, think that emotional singing stimulates both the sympathetic nervous system and the vagus nerve, which may help people get into a flow state.

In this study also, singing in unison, which is often done in churches and synagogues, increased HRV and vagus function.

However, no other similar studies were conducted. The study discussed above included only 15 healthy 18-year-olds. We don't know how different types of singing and chanting affect the vagus nerve in people of varying ages or with mental health problems. We need larger research.

In the only other study dealing with this connection, singing in professional as well as amateur singers was found to increase oxytocin.

After a singing session, both groups were energized but inexperienced singers said they had a greater sense of well-being and less enthusiasm than professionals. The writers pointed out that this may be because amateurs treated singing as a method of healing and self-realization while the practitioners were geared towards accomplishment.

So when singing and praying, you might want to relax and show yourself as much as possible. Try not to think about how you look, and whether you are going to achieve the targets that you set for that session.

3) Yoga

Limited studies suggest a connection between yoga and increased activity of the vagus nerve and parasympathetic system in general.

A 12-week yoga therapy was more closely associated with mood and anxiety improvements than walking exercises which served as the control group. The study found elevated levels of thalamic GABA, associated with improved mood and reduced anxiety.

Yoga is deemed good for the general mental and physical health service. More research is needed regarding its effects on the nerve tone of the vagus.

4) Meditation

Studies suggest that the vagus nerve could be stimulated indirectly by at least three types of meditation. In small studies, meditation on loving-kindness, meditation on mindfulness, and Om chanting improved variation in heart rate, which is consistent with vagal tone.

Some scientists believe this effect may be underpinned by deliberate, deep breathing which accompanies meditation and other contemplative practices. Attentive ventilation is hypothesized to specifically activate nerve vagus and nervous function in rest and digest.

Larger studies and more human studies are needed on the different types of meditation.

5) Positive Thoughts and Social Connection

Half of the participants were told in a survey of 65 people to sit down and think compassionately about others by silently repeating phrases such as "May you feel safe, may you feel happy, may you feel healthy, may you live with ease," and keep returning to those thoughts as their minds wandered.

The meditators showed an overall increase in positive emotions, such as joy, interest, amusement, serenity and hope after class, compared with the controls. As seen by heart rate variability, these emotional and psychological changes were correlated with a greater sense of connection to others and an improvement in vagal function.

Nevertheless, pure sleep did not always lead to a more toned vagus nerve. The change occurred only in meditators who became happier and felt more connected emotionally. Those who did just as much yoga but did not report feeling similar to others saw no improvement in the sound of the vagus nerve.

Given the need for more research, these findings suggest that the vagus nerve is related to how positive emotions and social connections will help people on a path to better health.

6) Deep and Slow Breathing

Deep and slow breathing is also hypothesized to stimulate the vagus nerve, and varying types of meditation, yoga, and relaxation techniques are likely common.

Your heart and neck contain neurons which have baroreceptors.

These neurons detect blood pressure and pass the neuronal signal to the brain (NTS). If a person has high blood pressure, this signal stimulates their vagus nerve, which binds to the heart to relieve blood pressure and heart rate. The result is less (sympathetic) fight-or-flight activation and more (parasympathetic) rest-and-digest activity.

Baroreceptors can be responsive to changing environments. Many scientists believe that the more alert they are, the more likely they can fire and warn the brain that the blood pressure is too high, and it's time to activate the vagus nerve to lower the pressure.

One research tested the effectiveness of yogic slow breathing on 17 healthy people, called ujjayi, which can be performed at varying breathing in and out speeds. Ujjayi breathing improved the sensitivity of baroreceptors and vagal stimulation, which lowered blood pressure, with a roughly equal amount of time breathing in and out.

This kind of sluggish respiration required 6 breaths a minute, which would be about 5 seconds per inhalation, 5 seconds per exhalation.

Some researchers believe that yogic slow breathing could also reduce anxiety by reducing the sympathetic nervous system and increasing the parasympathetic system, but that has not yet been confirmed.

Tip: Yoga teachers find out that gently, slowly, you need to relax. That means your belly should expand or go outwards when you breathe in. Your chest should be close in when you let it out. The more your belly expands, and the more you breathe, the more it cavities in.

7) Laughter

The saying "laughing is the best medicine" may have some truth. A couple of studies suggest the health benefits of laughing.

Scientists believe that laughter may activate the vagus nerve, suggesting laughter therapy may be effective for wellbeing. Yet there are still few experiments and it's hard to tell exactly how and why laughing makes us feel so good.

A study done on yoga laughter showed that the laughter community had improved HRV (heart rate variability).

There are different case studies, though, of people fainting from laughter. Physicians point out that this can be due to too much activation of the vagus nerve / parasympathetic system.

For example, some research suggests that fainting can happen after laughter, urination, coughing, swallowing, or bowel movements, all of which are helped by activation of the vagus.

There are case reports of people passing out of laughter having a rare syndrome (Angelman's) associated with increased stimulation of the vagus.

Laughter is also sometimes a side effect of stimulation of the vagus nerve which is done in children with epilepsy using special equipment.

Many people want to know if a healthy bout of humor is beneficial for cognitive function and defense against heart disease. Few studies suggest that laughter raises beta-endorphins and nitric oxide which the vascular system potentially protects.

8) Prayer

One small study found that reciting the rosary prayer could increase activation of the vagus. Specifically, cardiovascular rhythms appeared to improve, reducing diastolic blood pressure and increasing HRV.

According to one research group, reading one rosary cycle takes about 10 seconds, causing readers to breathe at 10-second intervals (including both in and out of breath), which increases HRV and thus vagus function.

9) PEMF

Many scientists speculate that magnetic fields can activate the vagus nerve. Pulsed Electromagnetic Field (PEMF) treatment improves heart rate variation and relaxation of the vagus in a study conducted on 30 healthy men. No other studies replicated those findings, however.

The PEMF devices are classified as products for general wellness. The FDA has not licensed them for treating any disease.

10) Probiotics

Emerging evidence indicates the gut microbiota has an effect on the brain. The gut's nervous system interacts with the brain via the vagus nerve, defined as "at the microbiota-gut-brain axis interface."

Some animal studies looked at the potential effects of probiotics on the vagus nerve but there is still a lack of clinical trials.

In an animal study, mice in response to the probiotic Lactobacillus rhamnosus reported some positive changes in GABA receptors mediated by the vagus nerve.

GABA receptors within the brain are involved in mood; a possible connection to L-stimulation of the vagus nerve gut. Rhamnosus and enhanced GABA activity adds the potential health benefits of probiotics to a set of emerging evidence.

11) Exercise

In animals, mild exercise stimulates gut flow – and activation of the vagus nerve was necessary to initiate this response. Some scientists hypothesize, thus, that exercise could activate the nerve of the vagus, although there is no clinical evidence to support it.

12)   Massage

You can stimulate the vagus nerve by massaging certain areas such as the carotid sinus (located on your neck). Research suggests reducing seizures can help. (Note: It is not advised to massage a carotid sinus at home due to possible fainting and other risks) A pressure massage may also stimulate the vagus nerve. These massages helped infants gain weight by stimulating the gut and this is believed to be largely mediated by activation of the vagus nerves.

Reflexology foot massages are also claimed to increase vagal activity and variability in heart rate while decreasing heart rate and blood pressure, according to one small study on healthy people and heart disease patients.

13) Fasting

Intermittent fasting and calorie reduction both increase animal heart rate variability which is thought to be a vagal tone marker.

Many people claim that intermittent fasting has increased their variation in heart rate, but no clinical trials can attest to that effect.

According to one theory, a reduction in metabolism might be mediated by the vagus nerve upon fasting. The vagus precisely senses a reduction in blood glucose and a decrease in mechanical and chemical input from the intestines. According to animal evidence, this would appear to increase vagus impulses from the liver to the brain (NTS), which reduces the metabolic rate.

Animal studies show that hormones like NPY are rising while CCK and CRH are decreasing during fasting.

The reverse can occur after feeding. Satiety-related stimulatory impulses from the intestines tend to lead to decreased sympathetic function and stress-responsiveness (higher CRH, CCK and lower NPY).

If starving, the vagus nerve will make the animals more responsive to estrogen. Fasting in female rats increases the number of receptors for estrogen in certain parts of the brain (NTS and PVN), which may be regulated by the vagus nerve.

14) Sleeping or Laying on Your Right Side

Limited studies suggest that reclining on your right side increases the variability of heart rate and vagal stimulation more than on other sides. For one test, sitting on the back contributed to the lowest activation of the vagus. We need more research.

15) Seafood (EPA and DHA)

The omega-3 fatty acids EPA and DHA improve heart rate variability (HRV) and reduce heart rate, according to several research studies. HRV is directly associated with a stimulation of the vagus nerve.

Several scientists believe that vagus nerve activation may explain why fatty acids of omega-3 are good for the heart, but more research is needed.

Fish is also an important part of the lectin preventive diet.

16) Zinc

Zinc increased stimulation of the vagus in rats fed a zinc-deficient 3-day diet. It is a very common mineral not getting enough of by some people.

17) Acupuncture

Traditional acupuncture points can stimulate the vagus nerve, especially the ones on the ears, according to limited research.

It is not always safe to get acupuncture. For one case, a man died from being too weak of a heart rate after vagus nerve stimulation. Make sure you work with a qualified practitioner in acupuncture and let your doctor know if you plan to see an acupuncturist.

18) Eating Fiber

GLP-1 is a satiating hormone that stimulates the brain's vagus impulses, slows down the movement of the intestines and makes us feel fuller after meals. Animal research indicates fiber can be a healthy way to boost GLP-1.

BREATHING EXERCISES

The first and most effective way of having a positive effect on your vagus nerve is to learn to breathe properly. Simply put, fast, shallow breathing of the chest is a sign of stress that activates the sympathetic branch while slow, deep breathing of the belly is a sign of rest that activates the vagus nerve.

If we want to know the easiest, most secure, and most effective way of breathing, then we need to look to the pioneers and examples who exist among us. Find some of the best artists of our day, vocal and instrumental. If you've ever been to a concert or opera, you've probably noticed that outstanding singers and instrumentalists can sing a whole set of songs without much of a break. In songs recorded by greats like Frank Sinatra, Aretha

Franklin, and Celine Dion, the singers never sound like they're out of breath or unable to hold a note because they've been practicing their breathing patterns. Opera singers are some of the most effective breathers on the planet; they have learned to control their diaphragm function while keeping their vocal muscles vibrating.

High-performing professional athletes are yet another category to remember. These are the best of the best— the ones that are not crumbling under pressure. Stars like Michael Jordan, Tom Brady, Cristiano Ronaldo, Tiger Woods, Wayne Gretzky, Nolan Ryan, Ken Griffey Jr., and Babe Ruth all had one thing in common — they all managed to control their stress levels by ensuring that their breath patterns remained optimal while they were performing. To perform at such high levels, these performers trained themselves by using a slow, calm, and comfortable breathing pattern to remain calm under high stress circumstances. You can also learn how to create an effective breathing pattern that can signal to your body that you are not under stress, thereby allowing for better communication through the vagus nerve and parasympathetic nervous system.

Multiple research findings have shown that sluggish breathing movements are highly effective in improving variation in heart rate. One study showed that slowing your breath rate for five minutes to six full breaths per minute was effective at immediately raising HRV. The effect on HRV is even more successful if this is individualized. Determining the ideal slow breath rate and feeling right for you personally will have the biggest positive impact on your HRV ratings.

To practice this exercise, here are simple steps:

- Sit up straight without allowing your back to rest against anything.
- Exhale and expel all the air from your lungs entirely.
- On your stomach, place your right hand and your left hand on your abdomen, just above your belly button.
- Take a deep breath of five to seven seconds through your nose, allowing only your belly to rise (feeling your left hand rising only).
- Hold that breath for two to three seconds.
- Exhale through your mouth for six to eight seconds, causing your stomach to sink (since your left hand just falls).
- Hold your breath for two or three seconds, without any air going into your lungs.
- Repeat steps 4 to 7 as many times as you feel comfortable or for a given time period.

Take five minutes per day to practice your own deep belly breathing and your body will be grateful. Perform this practice multiple times a day for best results, particularly during stressful periods. Just one minute of concentrating on steady, deep breathing can have significant positive impacts on your mood, levels of stress and overall health. Try to center your energy on breathing through your nose instead of your mouth to make this technique even more effective as you do it.

GETTING GREAT SLEEP

We both know the significance of having a good night's rest. Here, I'll give you some tools to use as part of a bedtime routine to increase the chances of a healthy, restful sleep night. A restful night of sleep has been shown to enhance autonomic stability by tests of heart rate variability.

- **Eliminate Blue Light Exposure in the Evenings**

Throughout the day the light wavelengths change and our bodies have adapted to their signals. As morning sun rises, in the red / yellow range, light is quite dry. By noon, the light is much brighter and more blue. Once again, in the evenings, the light turns towards a red / yellow hue when the sun is setting. These are the signals our body uses to tell us the current time of day, and which hormones and signals to secrete at precise times.

Our screens all emit a blue wavelength of light, including the laptop, TV, phone, and tablet. If we look at our screens right before bed every evening, we send a signal to our bodies that the time really is noon. This will slow down the release of melatonin, which is an important hormone needed to help us relax and fall asleep. Some devices now come with blue-light filters built in, but most do not.

To reduce blue light exposure while still using devices and screens during the evenings, you can:

- Enable Night Shift on your Apple devices
- Download the Twilight app on Android devices
- Download f.lux or Iris on your computer (Mac or Windows)
- Use blue-blocking sunglasses if you are watching the television

It is advised to use the TrueDark Twilight sunglasses for blue-blocking glasses which are the gold standard in blue-light blocking technology.

Instead of looking at your screen at night, reading a physical book or spending device-free time with loved ones or friends is recommended, since social connectivity is another great way to improve the function of the vagus nerve.

- **Shut Off Electronics at Night**

One of the best things you can ever do for your health is to cancel your subscription to Cable TV. It forces you at night, to stop watching TV. Also take steps to reduce computer use in the evenings and nights and, having done so, you will get noticeably better sleep.

Opening your computers like a cell phone or a laptop in a different room, turning off Wi-Fi routers with an automated timer and even placing your devices in flight mode are perfect ways to stop using them at night.

- **Don't Eat or Drink Too Late**

Bathroom breaks at night also throw off restful sleep. Whether you eat or drink later in the evening, then you're making your body ready to use the bathroom at night. Instead, have at least two hours of your final meal before you eat and your last drink of water at least one hour before bedtime. The next day, thank you for your waistline and your energy levels.

- **Love Your Space**

Sleeping in a clean, organized space is essential to improve the quality of your sleep and your health. You can't help but go to sleep when your bedroom is a mess, thinking about the cleaning and organizing that needs to be done. This negative energy gets into your consciousness and makes your sleep disturbed, which is simply added tension to your body and a simple way to turn off the night-time parasympathetic recovery system.

Have a feng shui assessment done on your space to ensure that it is organized in an energy-positive manner that will help you feel great and make you grow. Make sure you regularly clean and arrange your room, as this will have a direct effect on your mood and energy levels.

- **Sleeping on Your Side**

A 2008 study published in Circulation Journal by Yang et al. compared the HRV levels of the various sleep positions. The study was conducted to determine the best position for coronary artery disease patients compared to those without any blockages in their coronary arteries. The researchers found lying on your back are the worst position for HRV rates, both for patients in study and monitoring, while lying on either side showed significant change in HRV. Most notably, it has been found that sleeping on the right side is the better for vagal modulation, particularly within the control group.

What this essentially means is that sleeping on your back, or lying on your back for a longer period of time, will have negative effects on vagus nervous function, whereas lying on either side (right side preferred) would actually allow you to improve vagus nerve tone. This is because the airway is more likely to close when you are lying on your back, because your tongue will fall backwards due to the gravity force. That's not almost as easy when you're lying on your side. Note, an open airway is absolutely vital to breathing efficiency, both in terms of breath rate and breath distance.

COLD EXPOSURE

Have you ever jumped into a lake or swimming pool, only to realize that the water is cold and freezes you to your core? Your teeth start chattering, and your body starts shivering uncontrollably. The wind, too, is completely out of control. They take extremely shallow breaths so the diaphragm can't rest enough to settle down and breathe deeply.

As you can imagine this scenario is great to activate your sympathetic nervous system and the response to fight or flight. In the short term, your body is struggling to survive, and that has an immediate effect on how your body reacts. Your breath becomes shallow and fast, your heart rate increases and during this time your body does not wish to digest optimally. All that short-term action is meant for life.

What you might be surprised to hear is that this in turn has the amazing long-term effect of stimulating the parasympathetic nervous system. Continuous extreme cold or cryotherapy treatment helps you to control your intake, which has a positive overall effect on the function of the vagus and major anti-inflammatory activity throughout the body.

Periodic exposure to cold is one of the best and easiest ways to activate a lost vagus nerve and heal it. The easiest way to embed this into your life is to add cold exposure to your showers. One great tip is to take a normal shower, then turn the temperature down to the coldest possible at the end of the shower and let it hit you on the head and back of your neck for the last minute of your shower. It will be shocking to your system initially, and will change the way you breathe. During this time the goal is to work and regulate your body and take as many deep belly breaths as possible. If you can prepare your body to breathe through the air, the vagus nerve will become very powerful and the body will have a parasympathetic nervous system and vagus nerve functioning optimally. As this minute gets easier, you can add one to two minutes of cold exposure per week until you spend your entire shower in ice-cold water and there's a huge smile on your face!

Cryotherapy is an advanced and validated technique which is used through the parasympathetic nervous system to help reduce inflammation and enable healing. After each game or performance, the vast majority of the professional athletes, as well as performers like Tony Robbins, use cryotherapy. Mr. Robbins swears for his own health and considers it to have great curing effects.

For its amazing healing benefits even Wim Hof, the creator of the Wim Hof method, incorporates cold exposure in this method. He is known as the Iceman, as he frequently participates with his clients in ice baths and lectures about the effects of cold exposure. If you find like cold showers have become repetitive and too quick, try going out in just a pair of shorts and boots for a walk on a mountainside. A search for Wim on a Google image would show him doing just that.

HUMMING OR CHANTING

Another way of activating your vagus nerve is to stimulate and utilize the volunteer muscles it signals. By stimulating these muscles, you activate the centers of the brainstem which send signals through the vagus— not just the centers of muscle control, but also all the others around it.

You can activate the laryngeal muscles by humming and chanting which gets signals directly from the VN's superior and recurring laryngeal branches. We allow tightening and loosening of our vocal cords depending on muscle tension, thereby giving us a pitch level in our voices. When we practice deep humming in our throat, we activate and vibrate these muscles and stimulate the vagus to send out these signals.

Maybe you are aware of the sacred Hindu syllable "om" which is used when recited loudly to create a deep vibration in the throat. The "om" pulse, which is said to vibrate at the God's resonance point, has a strong spiritual connection in Hindu ism. Common terms such as Amin, Ameen, and Amen are used in many cultures; however they all seem to represent the word of god.

Vibrating at this frequency in the vagus nerve by chanting the word actually stimulates the throat and vocal cord laryngeal muscles, enabling stimulation of the VN motor fibers. If done long enough and with sufficient strength, it can be a powerful method of stimulating the other nerve signaling components. It allows us to control our breath, slow our thoughts and center ourselves to the point of extreme deep relaxation, and has been shown to improve the body's levels of digestion and inflammation. Before a meal, singing or repeating the word "Om" can be a perfect way to calm down, connect with the world and activate vagus nerve activity in the digestive tract and other visceral organs. After this stressful event, performing "om" during other occasions, including after a stressful event, is a valuable tool in reducing stress levels and sympathetic activation.

ACTIVATING GAG REFLEX

Activation of the gag reflex is another way of stimulating the muscles innervated by the VN along the same lines as humming and chanting. Otherwise known as the pharyngeal reflex, this reflex is required to protect us from choking, and requires a process of nerve stimulation to function optimally.

When an entity we do not know approaches our mouth and touches our soft palate (the sensitive part at the back of your mouth's roof), a very strong tactile impulse is sent through the ninth cranial nerve, up to the brainstem and to the motor portion of three different cranial nerves. The first of these nerves is the vagus' pharyngeal branch, which immediately contracts the three pharyngeal muscles at the back of the throat to stop the object from getting further into the body and potentially stuck in the airway. Often, the cranial nerve five and the cranial nerve twelve are activated, allowing the mouth to relax and the tongue to move the target outwards.

Activating the gag reflex actively would send an urgent warning to the vagus and other nerves to keep them communicating in a quick and efficient manner. The best time to do this is twice a day, when the teeth are being cleaned. The toothbrush can be used to touch the soft palate and stimulate that reflex. This is a nice, simple option proven to have a direct effect on VN signaling. Since we have a set of cranial nerves on either side of our body, it's necessary to stimulate the soft palate on both sides to get the full benefit of this exercise.

GARGLING

Gargling is the act of putting a sip of water in your throat open, then aggressively tossing it around. It involves activation of the three pharyngeal muscles at the back of the throat, and as such, it is another means of relaxing the vagus nerve by manipulating the muscle. Practicing this twice a day after brushing your teeth is a great way to easily harness this tool, as my father would consistently remind me.

Gargling with extra vigor, to the point that the eyes start to produce tears, is ideal for best results. It constantly sends signals from its brainstem nuclei while the vagus is fired, which cause the neighboring nuclei as they become larger. In this case, the superior salivary nucleus is stimulated which stimulates the glands around your eyes to produce tear-bearing fluid. If you gargle hard enough to make yourself tear, you do this properly and have a great effect on your vagus nervous system.

Adding any salt to the water you use to gargle, such as Himalayan pink salt, is a great option too. Gargling salt water has been shown to have antibacterial properties and may help the mouth and upper respiratory tract remove any harmful bacteria. The use of essential oils, like oregano oil, is another great option in your water, with very similar effects.

YOGA OR PILATES

Yoga and Pilates are not just about training the body but about soothing the mind and controlling the heart. Such approaches achieve maximum voluntary management of the body while through environmental stressors and showing you how to regulate the breath.

Most yoga sessions are booked with a slow breathing exercise to the deep belly. The idea is to help you to maintain your breath rhythm while keeping your body in different positions. Each of these positions involves a different type of physical stressor at the body. We've learned to use heat and humidity, which are even more rewarding, to increase the level of tension within this activity. Two examples of this are moksha and bikram yoga.

If we can continue to take a long, deep breath in the abdomen at times of stress, our bodies can function at much higher levels. If we train ourselves by keeping our breath to handle voluntary stressors, then we can be trained to maintain composure and handle other stressors with considerable ease.

If practiced with an emphasis on the heart, both yoga and Pilates are great tools to refine breathing patterns, enhance inflammatory responses, and activate the VN for optimum function.

MINDFULNESS PRACTICE

Do you take a moment to sit still before starting a task, close your eyes and focus your attention? Are you making sure you put 100 percent of yourself into the task at hand? Do you take a moment when you're resting to be grateful for your surroundings?

Exactly this is mindfulness: taking the time and making an effort to pay attention to what you are doing and what is going on around you. Many of us are jumping from task to task, or putting out fire after fire without paying attention to what is happening around us. We are so caught up in our own minds that it is put on the backburner to pay attention to one single task and give it our full attention; it feels like a waste of time and effort to do that.

Practice mindfulness involves executing each task to your full potential, with 100 percent of your concentration focused on that task. It means taking in your surroundings, being aware of and grateful for everything that has brought you into that exact moment.

The capacity to exercise awareness cannot occur when we are stressed out, inflamed and in pain. Our sympathetic nervous system has a tendency to capture our attention and prevent us from focusing on what we do. If you're actively practicing awareness throughout the day, you're focusing on your breath and how each task at hand can be achieved. This shifts the balance to the parasympathetic nervous system and enables the VN to perform its work.

Approaching a task deliberately involves doing one thing with full attention at a time and completing it before going on to the next task. Eating conscientiously enables you to feel satiated and not overeat. Paying attention to relaxation allows you to feel rested and rejuvenated sooner than you would imagine. All of these require a healthy and activated vagus nerve, as we must be able to rely on it so that our bodies can relax, digest and heal. Multi-tasking is the very opposite of being mindful.

LAUGHTER AND SOCIAL CONNECTEDNESS

If you knew that laughing would make your health healthier, would you do so more often? The last time you've had a good bonding session with colleagues, remember. Did you feel fantastic about the next few hours? Did you sleep that night any better? Have you awakened the next morning, feeling great?

Repeated ongoing research reveals laughing and humor yoga to be very successful in boosting variation of mood and heart rate. When we laugh with vigor and enjoyment, we tend to use our diaphragms, and in turn we exercise our ability to control our breath rate and ensure that our breathing patterns can be normalized. This is vagus nerve exercise.

Making a regular occurrence of vigorous laughter is a great and very enjoyable way to improve the vagus nerve function. Make it a point to watch funny videos or comedy shows as often as possible to feel socially connected, and to enjoy the health benefits of laughing. Taking laughing yoga classes in your community, meeting regularly with friends to exchange fun stories, and turning on a comedy film are all great options for more laughter. Social connectivity is directly involved with this because when we are in the presence of others, especially friends and family, we are more likely to laugh out loud. Social connectivity is one of health's greatest determinants, and may be even more important than the food you eat.

People would like to be around others. When we feel lonely and disconnected from others, we both have a negative effect on our mood and health. We tend to enjoy others' company, and like to have face-to-face interactions with real people. We tend to laugh more when we're around others, smile more and feel more relaxed.

When you feel lonely, sad, or just alone, you'll find a way to spend time with others and connect with people with similar values. If physical fitness is a significant value, join a gym or take part in a yoga class with friends. If communication is a significant value to you, join a group of toastmasters and practice your public speaking skills with supportive, like-minded people. If you value quality time with others, then go to a movie or a friendly meal to have a great time and converse. On the planet there are 8 billion people, and countless activities and interactions that enable you to connect with these people.

LISTENING TO MUSIC

After listening to some great music and singing along do you not feel really good? This is because your body actually feels relaxed during and after this time, and is able to perform recovery processes. It's the same reason that we enjoy belting our favorite tunes into the lyrics while waiting in our cars or stuck in traffic.

A 2010 research by Chuang et al. found that cancer patients who took part in a 2-hour music therapy session that included singing, listening, studying, and performing music showed significant improvements in levels of heart rate variability, and hence in vagus nerve and parasympathetic nerve functions. In 2014 another analysis by Lin et al. used HRV to demonstrate that the music of Mozart would enhance the activity of the parasympathetic nerve. Much of this research was done on children who were diagnosed with epilepsy, a severe neurological condition. Listening to the music of Mozart, in particular the "K.448" sonata for two pianos by Mozart, shows a reduction in recurrence of seizures and brain changes.

Next time you sit in traffic and feel stressed that you are late for a meeting or a job, turn on some good music and let your body move and sing along with it. You will naturally feel more relaxed and less anxious and at the same time you will still be going to your appointment. Play Mozart in the background if you are at home and feel out of it, and notice how you feel afterwards.

DAILY MOVEMENT OR EXERCISE

Our bodies are built for movement. Muscles are some of the body's most essential and most neglected muscles, and muscle cells are the best to help us regulate our levels of blood sugar and body fat— if we use them. The issue is that most of us are sitting and lacking movement every day for a very long time, and then sitting in the car, sitting on the couch, repeating this daily lack of movement.

Practicing some degree of movement, preferably one that helps increase your heart rate for a short period of time by increasing body stress levels, helps to improve parasympathetic nerve activity. There are times when both the sympathetic and parasympathetic systems can be activated, and one of those circumstances is recovery after exercise. During recovery, we optimize our breathing pattern, which increases signaling to the airway's muscles to increase patentability, trains the heart to become stronger, and pumps out more blood with each pump, and allows us to shift back to a regular parasympathetic condition.

Moving your muscles and getting your body to do things that stress it out on a daily basis will teach the body how to recover faster from the stress while also helping you balance energy levels and sources of macronutrient fuel. Use your muscles to make things happen on your body, preferably outdoors.

SUNLIGHT EXPOSURE

During the whole day exposure to sunlight is directly related to your sleep. Our bodies are genetically programmed to work according to the amount and type of sunlight that falls into our eyes and skin. It has a direct effect on the way we operate at a cellular level. If we spend a whole day indoors with limited exposure to true sunlight under artificial lighting, we are depriving our cells of optimal signaling and function.

During daytime duration is directly associated with increased levels of HRV. During sunrise and sunset, our eyes and skin prefer to receive signals from red, infrared, and yellow wavelengths, while at mid-day they prefer blue, green, violet, and ultraviolet light. Obviously, Sun exposure will do this, while our offices, vehicles, and houses won't–at least not yet. At the time of this writing, many companies are developing the Circadian lighting technology.

Since sunlight is directly linked to HRV levels, it is highly recommended that you get outdoors and get direct sunlight every day on your skin. An even better option is to do this at several different times of the day. Within 30 minutes of sunrise, two or three times during the day and within 30 minutes of sunset, the best times to get outside are. Better still, spend the whole day outdoors whenever possible. If your body senses the sunrise and is pre-conditioned to the UV light that we experience during the day, you are far less likely to burn your skin during the day.

SUPPLEMENTATION

Because our diets lack nutrient density and our environments have reduced our diversity of microbiomas, supplementation is a smart way to ensure that our cells get the right micronutrients and signals to enable them to function optimally. Contrary to previous belief, supplements aren't a waste of money, as long as the right person takes them for the right reason. We can determine the best supplements for each individual to reach their optimal cellular function using functional laboratory testing. Nonetheless, there are some essential foods and vitamins for the signaling that can benefit us all. Note that this is for general advice. You should talk to your primary health care practitioner before starting or stopping any prescribed or recommended medications or supplements.

PROBIOTICS

Antibiotic use, C-sections, and poor nutrient density diets have led us to have poor bacterial diversity in our gut and low levels of good bacteria. Checking to validate which bacterial species are present is the best choice but most of us will need to use probiotics to help our gut and skin microbiome. Probiotics are externally occurring bacteria. We will help improve the bacterial diversity and establish healthy bacterial colonies when swallowed. These are different from prebiotics, which are usually derived from fiber and act as the bacteria's food for us to produce vitamins and minerals.

I recommend spore-based, naturally formed bacterial species such as Bacillus which are naturally formed in soil when choosing a probiotic. These probiotics fill in the voids left when other bacteria die. Probiotics that need to be cooled tend to have a very low absorption rate (5 to 10 per cent) compared to spore-based probiotics and those that need not be cooled.

For most patients on a maintenance protocol MegaSporeBiotic is my preferred probiotic option. It has a very high rate of absorption, it does not need to be refrigerated, and it includes Bacillus species that can help fill the voids created by many different types of deficient bacterial species, not just

Lactobacillus and Bifidobacteria, which are the main species protected by most probiotics.

OMEGA-3 FATTY ACIDS

High-quality omega-3 fatty acids are not found in our low nutrient density diets and Standard American Diets. Often referred to as fish oils, they are most commonly derived from fish, but can also come from some plant sources, which are the preferred vegan source.

The problem with most ingestible omega-3 oils is that they are formed artificially from the natural sources and this processing decreases the efficacy of these sources. The natural form contains triglycerides whilst ethyl esters are present in the processed form. Ethyl esters tend to taste and smell far catchier than triglycerides.

I highly recommend going for the triglyceride type when choosing a high-quality source of omega-3 fatty acids, as it is natural and contains a high amount of EPA and DHA, both of which are necessary for brain function and anti-inflammatory effects in the body. EPA and DHA improve the function of the nerves, including VN function, as they are necessary for nerve myelination and provide anti-inflammatory effects. Also recently, supplementation with omega-3 fatty acids has been shown to improve variability in the heart rate in obese children.

5-HTP FOR SEROTONIN

This segment is unique to addressing depressed mood and stress issues. Sadly, depression and mental health issues are very prevalent in North America today, and evidence has shown that antidepressant drugs can actually cause more of a problem. A long-term study published in 2014 by O'Regan et al. found that there was a decreased HRV in people with depression, and that these effects are potentially increased by anti-depressant medications that try to improve serotonin levels.

The serotonin precursor is termed 5-HTP. It can be used as an important supplement helping the body to build up its own serotonin. Most depression cases are due to serotonin imbalance, and organic acid functional testing, which I use with almost every patient entering my office, can actually tell our patients if they have too much serotonin and use it very quickly, or if they are running low in their production.

One thing to remember is that the vast majority of serotonin production is assisted by the intestinal microbiome. A balanced microbiome produces a good amount of serotonin and allows a balanced mood while an unbalanced microbiome does the opposite, leading to an increased risk of mental health problems.

CHAPTER 5

PASSIVE METHODS TO ACTIVATE THE VAGUS NERVE

Besides all the active exercises you can perform on your own, there are passive treatments that can have profound effects on vagus nerve activation. Some of these involve using certain equipment or visiting a health care provider while others can be done in your own home comfort. Before beginning any kind of treatment, remember to discuss these options with your primary health care provider.

Auricular Acupuncture

A substantial and increasing body of research indicates that in many patients with depression, anxiety, epilepsy, LPS-induced inflammation, tinnitus, and highly active pain receptors, acupuncture and transcutaneous vagus nerve stimulation through the auricular branch of the VN produce positive results. The best part about this form of treatment is that it is efficient without invasive action.

There is also a growing trend within the health care sector focused on vagus nerve activation by electrical stimulation. This is done by implanting an electrical stimulator on the vagus nerve itself, surgically. Acupuncture is considerably safer than this invasive procedure, and just as effective. In fact, the exact same neural pathways involve auricular acupuncture and implanted vagus nerve stimulation devices.

Visceral Manipulation

Visceral manipulation (VM) is a less common therapy but one that is highly effective when correctly practiced. Typically practiced by osteopaths, chiropractors, naturopaths, and other health care providers, VM is the gentle physical manipulation of the abdomen's organs, thereby increasing the flow of blood to areas that do not function best. Once learnt right, patients can use this feedback device on their own.

As we know, all abdominal organs including the liver, gallbladder, pancreas, kidneys, spleen, stomach, small intestine, and ascending and transverse sections of the large intestine are innervated by the vagus nerve. For the VN to influence these organs and communicate organ function to the brain, proper functionality of the organs is essential. In these organs physical restrictions can build up which can only be altered by physical manipulation and mobilization. Improving the blood flow to these organs can have major beneficial organ health outcomes and allow the VN to send out optimum function-related signals.

Gently administered hands-on treatment is used by visceral stimulation practitioners to find areas of changed or reduced activity within the viscera to remove constraints within these visceral organs. The treatment involves a gentle compression, mobilization or soft tissue elongation. Having a licensed visceral stimulation specialist in your region may be a good idea, especially for those with detoxification disorder or liver, gallbladder or kidney discomfort.

Electrical Stimulation

Researchers have performed experiments in the last hundred or so years to learn about the symptoms of the vagus nerve. One technique involved stimulating the VN on experimental animals with the aid of electrical stimulators. In addition to learning about the value of the VN itself, researchers eventually determined that they were able to supplement its functions by electrically stimulating the vagus nerve.

Experiments were done in the 1980s and early 1990s to show that vagus stimulation in the neck was effective in reducing seizure activity in dogs. This research resulted in dedicated clinical trials which produced devices for vagus nerve stimulation (VNS) that could be implanted into the neck. The FDA approved these devices for the treatment of epilepsy in 1997, and for the treatment of chronic, treatment-resistant depression in 2005. Regarding various medical problems, including insomnia, bipolar disorder, treatment-resistant anxiety disorders, Alzheimer's disease, and obesity, laboratories and companies have been developing and enhancing tools to electrically activate the VN since. The most widely used clinically electrical VNS system currently is the Cyberonics NCP Program, which is inserted during an outpatient procedure on the left vagus nerve. This unit is used for treating patients with severe depression and/or epilepsy resistant to the treatment.

Right-side VNS is effective in animal models of epilepsy and seizures but strong effects on depressive symptoms are not known. Preliminary human trials are promising and have produced positive effects, and some firms have already started to create vagus nerve stimulation tools that can be used for different conditions. BioControl Medical's CardioFit system uses right-side VNS to activate efferent fibers and help in heart failure treatment, while BioControl Medical's FitNeSS system is designed to activate afferent fibers, thereby helping to reduce the side effects of electrical vagal stimulation.

Typical surgical risks associated with this procedure include infection, pain, scarring, swallowing difficulties and paralysis of the vocal cord. Side effects of implanted electrical stimulators include voice changes, heaviness, sore throat, cough, headache, chest pain, breathing problems (especially during exercise), difficulty swallowing, abdominal pain, nausea, skin tingling, insomnia, and bradycardia (heart rate slowing). Though many of these may be temporary, they may be severe, and may last forever.

There are other electrical stimulation systems which do not need to be implanted, but they have mixed results and are only licensed at this stage for certain conditions. Cerbomed's NEMOS system is a transcutaneous VNS unit, applied to the vagus-innervated portion of the body. Currently it has been cleared for epilepsy and depression treatment in Europe. In Europe, gammaCore device from the US-based company electroCore has been granted clearance for acute treatment of headaches in clusters, migraines and overuse of headaches by medication. The gammaCore is a portable handheld device with two flat contact surfaces for stimulation that are applied over the vagus nerve to the neckside. Larger trials for treating other conditions are underway.

DAILY PRACTICES FOR ACTIVATING THE VAGUS NERVE

- **Gargling 2x daily**: Keep a cup next to your sink. Use it to gargle your teeth twice a day, in the morning and at night.

- **Gag reflex activation 2x daily:** Use your toothbrush to activate the gag reflex on both the left and right side of your soft palate, as you brush your teeth in the morning and at night.

- **Humming 2x daily:** Practice humming deep in your mouth during your daily commute, or to book your day. You can use the term "om" to keep the pulse as long as you can exhale in your throat.

- **Cold shower 1x daily:** End your daily shower with cold water for one minute (as cold as possible) and practice breathing through the temperature change shock. As that becomes easier, increase the time every three days by 30 to 60 seconds until all of your shower is taken under cold water.

- **Deep breathing 3x daily:** Before each meal, perform three to five minutes of deep breathing in a still room. This will help calm you down for each meal and improve your digestion.

- **Sunlight exposure 3x daily:** Go outside and expose your skin to the sun within 30 minutes of sunrise, in the middle of the day and within 30 minutes of sunset, at least five minutes each time. If you live in a colder climate, expose your eyes to light for two to three minutes at each of these times and practice breathing through the cold whenever you do so.

- **Sleep on your side each night:** Put a pillow in between your knees to prevent you sleeping at night on your side.

CHAPTER 6

MEASURING VAGUS NERVE FUNCTION

We will discuss the different methods used in this chapter to measure vagus nerve function and determine whether the VN is functioning optimally or needs training. These methods are the measurement of variability in heart rate, heart rate, breath pattern and transit time in the bowel. The most important thing to keep in mind is that one can change anything that can be measured. When you check the vagus nerve output and it isn't ideal at the time, you'll be able to activate it and improve the work when you make the effort to do so individually.

Heart Rate Variability

Heart rate variability (HRV) is the gold standard for assessing the activity of the vagus nerve. Any single measure is known to represent the activity levels of the vagus nerve and vagal tone in a better and more accurate way. It is measured most accurately in a laboratory setting using very expensive and sophisticated equipment; however we can measure it at home with a good amount of accuracy with reasonable investment.

Note the vagus nerve has the purpose of slowing down and controlling the heart rate to a comfortable pace of rest. There are four chambers in the heart: the left and right atria, through which the blood reaches the heart; and the left and right ventricles, which pump the blood into the blood vessels so that it can reach the rest of the body around it.

A pounding heart's "lub-dup" in turn reflects the two stages of the heartbeat. The first heart pump— the "lub" portion — represents the operation of the left and right atria's muscular walls, pumping blood into the ventricles. This process reflects the stronger ventricular walls pumping blood into the aorta and pulmonary artery, delivering oxygenated blood to the body's cells, and deoxygenated blood to the lungs. After the "lub-dup," there is a short period of time called an "interbeat interval," during which there is no expected electrical activity in the heart.

Heart rate variability is the time measurement, in milliseconds, between successive heart pumps — the time from the end of one "lub-dup" to the start of the next "lub-dup." An important indicator of both cardiovascular and autonomic health is whether and how much the time between pumps varies. The more active your vagus nerve will be, the lower your heart rate will be within an optimal zone and the more variable the time between your heart pumps will be.

If your heart had no parasympathetic or sympathetic nerves to inside it, it would pump at about 100 beats per minute (bpm). Sympathetic innervation will increase heart rate to about 120 bpm. A heart rate around 120 bpm is quite high and means that about two heart beats occur each second. This means that between each stroke of your heart there'll be between 400 to 450 milliseconds of time. One would find this to be weak HRV, as the time between pumps remains relatively constant— the gap between beats is at most 38 milliseconds.

In comparison, parasympathetic innervation helps to lower heart rate and improve variation in heart rate. HRV can be measured to determine how healthy a person really is and how well their vagus nerve is firing when the heart rate drops down to its normal resting state. The optimum heart rate is between 50 and 70 bpm, and the HRV will vary considerably between pumps. This would be considered an example of high variability in heart rate, since there are 130 milliseconds of variation between beats. The higher the amplitude of your heart rate, the more likely you will have a higher fitness level, cardiovascular health and vagal tone. Strong HRV is one of the best lifespan predictors, as well.

As technology is improving and becoming available to the general public, instruments are emerging that allow us to take control of our health and measure these health predictors on our own.

Resting Heart Rate and Heart Rate Recovery

Resting your heart rate is a simple measurement which tells you how well your body is working. If we consider that the average resting heart rate is generally between 60 and 100 bpm but without any autonomic stimulation the heart rate would be about 100 bpm, it is safe to extrapolate that the lower your heart rate within the optimal range, the stronger the parasympathetic signaling to the heart.

The optimal heart rate should be in the region of 50 to 70 bpm in a healthy person. Many athletes tend to find their heart rate at the lower end, 50 to 60 bpm, while less active but still healthy individuals tend to be 60 to 70 bpm in heart rate. New research shows that a heart rate that rests above 76 bpm is associated with increased risk of heart attack. In fact, there is a correlation between the risk of dying from any cause and an increase in heart rate in both men and women. Essentially the higher the chance of dying from any cause, especially one that is cardiovascular, as the resting heart rate increases.

It is important to measure how quickly your heart rate gets back to its resting rate after exercise. High-intensity exercise and conditioning are known to reduce the resting heart rate over time, and regular training is correlated with faster recovery times. If after an exercise session it takes you a long time to recover, this is a sign of poor cardiovascular health and poor vagal tone; remember, vagus signaling is needed to slow heart rate and keep heart rate resting. Optimal recovery from exercise involves a drop of 12 bpm per minute, whereas unhealthy individuals take longer and tend to be less than 12 bpm downwards.

To calculate improvement of heart rate, monitor the heart rate a few times while you are comfortable. You can use a mobile or wearable technology to locate and monitor the number with reasonably precision. Then, perform your normal exercise or training routine and test your heart rate immediately at the end of the session, using the same method as before. After 2 minutes, 4 minutes, and 6 minutes, test again. Your heart rate should drop by more than 24 bpm after 2 minutes, by more than 48 bpm after 4 minutes, and should be very close to your original resting heart rate after 6 minutes. This depended, of course, on how intensive the exercise was, and whether it was aerobic (e.g. running) or anaerobic (e.g. weight lifting).

When you routinely monitor your heart rate and HRV, you'll find a rise in HRV during exercise; the vagus nerve is highly active during rehabilitation as it tries to rebuild tissues. If exercises and tones muscles, heart, and spinal nerves in aerobic and anaerobic training, then recovery is the training session for the vagus nerve. The more you train, the more you recover and the more efficiently your vagus nerve will fire when you exercise next time. This is why recovery rates are improving for those who regularly exercise: the VN is practicing for greater efficiency and sound to perform their job.

Paradoxical Breathing Pattern Test

Do you use your diaphragm to start breathing? Have your breathing patterns become irregular and your vagus nervous system worked less than optimally? This is a very simple test and a tool for training yourself to breathe with your diaphragm.

Sit in a chair straight up, or lay down on the floor with your legs. Place the center of your chest with your right hand and place your left hand in the center of your belly. Now give in a deep breath. If your right hand works more than your left hand, then you breathe poorly. Our bellies should rise and fall more during the inhalation process than our chest does, so if we are breathing well our left hand will rise and fall more than our right hand.

Most people will find that their abdomen moves more than their stomach. This is a sign of paradoxical breathing and shows that somebody probably doesn't use their diaphragm to breathe fully, deeply and properly. When you breathe paradoxically, don't panic, because you can teach yourself to once again be an efficient breather. It'll just take some effort and a daily practice to relearn patterns you had when you were a kid a long time ago.

Sesame Seed Bowel Transit Time Test

How well is food moving within your digestive tract? Does that travel at an optimum, healthy pace? The sesame seed bowel transit time test will give us some insight about how our digestive tract functions, and if we need to make any health changes. All you need is a tablespoon of golden or yellow sesame seeds, a cup of tea, a watch or clock, and a notepad and a pen.

We know our gut lacks the enzymes for digesting and breaking down sesame seeds (similar to corn), which is what makes them so effective for this test. We all learn that the vagus nerve is the peristalsis driving force that keeps the digestive tract going at an optimum rate. Any variations in this rate may signal a loss of control of VN or some other digestive dysfunctions.

Here's how to get the test done. First, add a cup of water to the sesame seeds and mix it around. First, drink the cup of water in it with sesame seeds, and be careful not to chew the seeds. Look at the time, and mark it on your notepad or computer. Then, wait until you have to go to the bathroom for a bowel movement next time. Each time you go to the toilet and have a bowel movement, take a look at your stools and see if you see any sesame seed. Label the times and start to search until you no longer see any egg. The optimal time to see the seeds start appearing is about 12 hours after ingestion and the latest is around 20 hours after ingestion. Seeing seeds after ingestion 16 hours suggests optimal digestive sequence and function.

If your body pushes the seeds out very quickly, your digestive tract will not work hard enough and the VN probably will not fir optimally. If your body is very sluggish in removing the seeds, then the operation of the vagus will definitely decrease. Testing the gut microbiome is highly recommended in either case, as it can reveal the cause of poor bowel transit time and potentially poor vagus nerve signaling.

CONCLUSION

Now that you understand the nature of the parasympathetic nervous system, and the degree to which knowledge is conveyed by the VN, the power is in your hands to enhance its function and restore your health. For some of you, these strategies and protocols will have profound effects that will dramatically improve your energy, digestion, inflammation and pain, while for others; this may simply be the first step on your journey.

Wherever you're on your health journey, take a moment to commit yourself to becoming responsible for it. Share it with those around you — family, friends, and loved ones— who need to hear that there's answers to what might ail them.

Keep up the good work and form healthier habits for those of you who make significant improvements with some of the simple changes outlined in this book! That's perfect for those who need someone to hold their hand through the ride, and nothing to feel ashamed of at all. Seek out forward-thinking practitioners of health care who do not practice in - the-box medicine. Choose someone who will genuinely care about you as a person and help you to find the root cause of your problems.

Printed in Great Britain
by Amazon